D1281655

BETWEEN *THE* *FLOOD* AND THE RAINBOW

Interpreting the Conciliar Process
of Mutual Commitment (Covenant)
to Justice, Peace
and the Integrity of Creation

Compiled by
D. Preman Niles

WCC Publications, Geneva

Cover design and photo: Rob Lucas

ISBN 2-8254-1085-3

© 1992 WCC Publications, World Council of Churches,
150 route de Ferney, 1211 Geneva 2, Switzerland

Printed in Switzerland

Contents

Introduction

Between the Flood and the Rainbow was the title of a document containing theological expositions, affirmations and covenant commitments which was prepared for the world convocation on "Justice, Peace and the Integrity of Creation" (Seoul, Republic of Korea, 5-12 March 1990). We have taken that title for this volume as well because, now as then, we seem to live between the flood and the rainbow, between the threat of disaster and world calamity on the one side and hope on the other.

The threat of a nuclear holocaust has diminished with the ending of the Cold War confrontation. It is a matter of serious concern, however, that other countries are attempting to buy the nuclear technology and instruments of the former USSR, which could lead to new situations for nuclear confrontation.

We rejoice with the nations of the former so-called Eastern bloc as they rid themselves of a totalitarian ideology which held them and their people in its grip for nearly half a century. But we are concerned that prominent political leaders in North America and Europe tout the collapse of the USSR and its influence as a victory for the free-market economic system, without acknowledging the fact that many nations in Latin America, the Caribbean, Africa, Asia and the Pacific are being crippled by the international debt burden which is a product of the very economic system they hold up as the underpinning for a new world order.

We are glad that the "Earth Summit" in Rio de Janeiro in June 1992 drew wide participation from world leaders and broad enthusiasm from people at the grassroots. We are thankful that it produced some agreements, commitments and conventions that begin to acknowledge the depth of the threats posed to the natural environment. But we are disappointed by the failures to reach agreement in some areas, the weakening of certain goals and the insufficient financing made available. And we remain concerned that the industrialized nations will try to hijack the follow-up to Rio in the interest of sustainable growth for the rich rather than sustainable development for all.

We celebrate with friends in South Africa the dismantling of the systems of apartheid. But we are worried that extremist white and black groups and some segments of the South African military are determined to derail the "peace process" by fomenting communal violence which has already claimed thousands of lives.

There are indeed hopeful signs of change, though the threats to justice, peace and the integrity of creation are still real. We continue to live between the flood and the rainbow: between the threats to life and God's promise of a new heaven and a new earth. It is therefore heartening to see the JPIC process gather momentum in many places, and manifest itself in many forms.

The world convocation on "Justice, Peace and the Integrity of Creation" was meant to be a major step as well as a major resource in the process. For many this has indeed been the case. But for others, especially in Europe, the convocation was not the watershed in the process that it was intended to be.

The final document from the convocation, "Now Is the Time", was brought out almost immediately after the event, so that a wider group of people could make their own judgment about what the convocation accomplished. This publication was to have been followed by a full report of the convocation with essays interpreting the process up to, including, and beyond the convocation.

Unfortunately, this ambitious project had to be abandoned. One of the problems was the lack of personnel and funds in the World Council of Churches. Another was the JPIC process itself. Surprisingly, it seemed to take on a life of its own, circumventing and even overcoming obstacles to reach new stages in its development. This tremendous movement, with its twists and turns, made it hard to decide on a convenient cut-off point for documenting and interpreting the JPIC. A pause has been provided with the JPIC being lodged in a new unit called "Justice, Peace and Creation" in the new programme structure of the WCC.

This volume is not a report of the convocation. Rather, it is a collection of essays which seek to interpret the conciliar process with all of its complexities. Some reflect directly on the convocation while others deal broadly with the conciliar process. All the essays are from persons who, in one way or another, were involved in the preparation for the world convocation. In that sense they provide an insider's understanding of the process as it developed, the ways in which it manifested itself in the convocation, and the tasks that lie ahead. The book is offered in the hope that it will help in the continuing JPIC process.

A historical account of the JPIC process from the sixth (Vancouver, 1983) to the seventh (Canberra, 1991) assembly, with an indication of the important decisions made at each point, charts, so to speak, "the official course of JPIC". It provides a background for the essays. Most of the important regional and global meetings on JPIC are also taken note of.

Section I deals with the achievements and failures of the process. Kässmann, Bührig and Hall reflect on the process leading to and including the world convocation. Reuver presents the worldwide JPIC process against which the contribution of the convocation needs to be evaluated. Ruiz-Perez and Noll provide two regional perspectives on the process. We would have liked to include more regional perspectives, but to wait for more contributions would have further delayed this publication.

Section II provides some responses to the process after the convocation. Kim reflects on the consequences for Asia and Williamson evaluates the impact of JPIC on the Canberra assembly of the World Council of Churches. For the Roman Catholic and Orthodox churches, the development of the preparatory process and even the convocation posed difficulties. Coste from a Catholic perspective and Limouris from an Orthodox perspective look at the problems and sketch possible ways in which their churches can participate in the continuing JPIC process.

Section III, under the heading "An Unfinished Agenda", looks at some of the unresolved issues in JPIC. In order not to slow down the preparatory process of the convocation, many theological and ecclesiological issues had to be left unresolved. All of these surfaced in one way or another at the convocation as points of tension. Best discusses these issues, and suggests how they may be clarified and resolved in ways that will strengthen the conciliar process. Oh's essay looks at the issues of justice, peace and the integrity of creation from the perspective of those who are the victims of injustice, violence and the degradation of the environment. It is the absence of this perspective that often leads to a betrayal of the vision of the conciliar process of mutual commitment (covenant) to justice, peace and the integrity of creation.

The document from the convocation, "Now Is the Time", is given as an appendix.

Were it not for the hard work of the preparatory group for the world convocation on "Justice, Peace and the Integrity of Creation" with the support of a small staff, much of what is now known as JPIC would not have happened. The preparatory group had in its membership persons from many church traditions (including the Roman Catholic Church), regional ecumenical organizations, Christian world bodies, and movements and groups for JPIC. From time to time, many persons freely gave of their time as consultants to help the work. We thank them all.

The member churches of the WCC in the Republic of Korea together with other churches who are members of the Korean Council of Churches were of immense help in organizing the world convocation in Seoul. A local JPIC preparatory group, under the leadership of Bishop Simon Kim and the Rev. Kwon Ho-kyung, worked under great pressure. We are grateful to all of them.

Dr Marga Bührig and Archbishop Walter Khotso Makhulu, presidents of the World Council of Churches, were moderator and vice-moderator of the preparatory group. With much patience and humour in difficult situations, they ably guided the work of the preparatory group. As a token of appreciation, this volume of essays is dedicated to them.

D. PREMAN NILES

A Historical Survey
of the JPIC Process

D. Preman Niles

There have been, and still continue to take place, a number of local and national JPIC events as high points of the conciliar process in those situations. These are far too numerous to document. Even those that have come to our attention, and may be documented, are only a small percentage of what is happening worldwide. We have heard of many of these second-hand either on our travels or when requests were made for resource materials. We will mention a few examples just to give an idea of what is going on.

A local church in the USA had declared a JPIC week culminating in a JPIC Sunday. Local as well as WCC JPIC materials were on display. This was reported to us by a WCC staff person who happened to visit this church. Another accidental discovery was that almost all of the resource materials on JPIC put out by the WCC were being translated into Indonesian for use in the churches. There have been many JPIC events in the nations of Europe. What surprised us most was the way in which the "Konziliar Prozess" functioned in the people's struggles for democracy, especially in the former German Democratic Republic and in Czechoslovakia.

Accessibility and adaptability, among other characteristics, constitute the genius of JPIC. In the final issue of the JPIC newsletter, *Forum*, published immediately after the world convocation, Margot Wahl, a JPIC staff person in the WCC, wrote: "It has been fascinating to observe how the commitment to JPIC has left the churches and the documents and is carried by the people. It is coming back to us now diversified and strengthened, because it is applied to a concrete struggle in different contexts." JPIC was and continues to be a people's process. It is this dynamism that initially challenged the churches and the instruments of the ecumenical movement at the Vancouver assembly, sustained the process through the convocation to the Canberra assembly, and still presses us to continue with the process.

The historical survey given below charts only the regional and global course of JPIC. It lists many of the principal JPIC events and provides a rough sketch of the way the process moved through the legislative bodies of the WCC. The intention is to provide an easy reference for seeing the way the conciliar process moved from the Vancouver (1983) to the Canberra (1991) assemblies of the WCC.

August 1982: The assembly of the World Alliance of Reformed Churches (WARC) issues statements on peace and justice requesting the urgent attention of churches to several global problems.

March 1983: The executive committee of WARC: "We dare to propose that all churches which confess Jesus Christ as God and Saviour... should form a covenant for peace and justice... In order to give visible expression to this covenant, we suggest, under the auspices of the World Council of Churches, the preparation and early summoning of a special ecumenical gathering in which all churches would participate and bear witness to ways of peace and justice."

July-August 1983: The sixth assembly of the World Council of Churches: "To engage member churches in a conciliar process of mutual commitment (covenant) to justice, peace and the integrity of all creation should be a priority for World Council programmes. The foundation of this emphasis should be confessing Christ as the life of the world and Christian resistance to the demonic powers of death in racism, sexism, caste oppression, economic exploitation, militarism, violation of human rights, and the misuse of science and technology." See also the assembly statement on peace and justice and the issues for the churches report on "Struggling for Justice and Human Dignity". Delegates to the assembly from the churches in the German Democratic Republic ask the WCC to convene a council for peace.

July-August 1985: The central committee of the WCC officially launches the JPIC process in the WCC. Requests that JPIC continue the work done on the study for a "Just, Participatory and Sustainable Society". Asks for clarification on "covenanting" and "integrity of creation". Encourages collaboration with the Roman Catholic Church. Calls for support for national and regional initiatives like a council for peace in Europe. Requests a broad-based dialogue on JPIC to include perspectives from indigenous people, women, youth, other faiths and the scientific community. Approves the formation of an advisory group on JPIC in the WCC and recommends the holding of a world conference on "Justice, Peace and the Integrity of Creation".

March 1986: The executive committee of the WCC accepts a staff report on JPIC which outlines proposals for the programmatic work of JPIC in the Council and appoints a JPIC advisory group.

November 1986: JPIC consultation on "covenanting". Also, first meeting of the JPIC advisory group. It does not clarify "covenanting" but says that it is one of many terms that may be used to express the commitment of the churches. The consultation calls for a world convocation. It avoids the term "council", since the time for holding a council of the church in the strict sense of the term has not come. But there can be a "world convocation" through which the churches could express their common witness to justice, peace and the integrity of creation.

January 1987: The central committee of the WCC receives and debates the report from the JPIC consultation. Much time spent in trying to clarify the theological and ecclesiological issues raised by JPIC, though with little success. The committee says: "The 1990 world convocation for 'Justice, Peace and the Integrity of Creation' is a decisive step towards fulfilling the mandate of the sixth assembly of the WCC in Vancouver. It marks an important stage on the road towards common and binding pronouncements and actions on the urgent questions of survival of humankind." It decides to invite the Roman Catholic Church to be a "co-inviter" for the convocation and requests the general secretary to forward the invitation to the Vatican.

September 1987: The WCC executive committee receives the strong recommendation of Unit II, Justice and Service, expressed through its moderator, regarding the need to include the movements for justice, peace and the integrity of creation in the JPIC process, now largely become a church-centred process. The executive committee decides that the world convocation should have representatives from the churches, participating organizations and other advisers, totalling 500 persons.

October-November 1987: Inter-Orthodox consultation on the integrity of creation meets in Sofia, Bulgaria, and issues the document "Orthodox Perspectives on Creation".

December 1987: WCC general secretary receives letter from Johannes Cardinal Willebrands, president of the Pontifical Council for Promoting Christian Unity, saying that the Roman Catholic Church is unable to accept the invitation to be a co-inviter for the convocation, at the same time expressing the desire "to collaborate with the World Council of Churches in this important project as much as we possibly can". The Roman Catholic Church agrees to have persons on the preparatory group for the world convocation and a staff person for JPIC in the WCC.

March 1988: Consultation on the integrity of creation held in Granvollen, Norway, with participants representing Protestant, Orthodox and Catholic churches, other faith communities, indigenous people, women and youth. It issues a statement, "Integrity of Creation: An Ecumenical Discussion" to engage churches, Christian groups and all people who are concerned about the issue, in a process of study and action.

March 1988: The WCC executive committee says: "The purpose of the world convocation will be to make theological affirmations on justice, peace and the integrity of creation and to identify the major threats to life in these three areas and show their interconnectedness; and make and propose to the churches acts of mutual commitment in response to them." It appoints the preparatory group for the world convocation, and extends an invitation to Christian world bodies and regional ecumenical organizations to have at least one representative on the preparatory group. It appoints two of the presidents of the WCC, Dr Marga Bührig and Archbishop Walter Khotso Makhulu, as moderator and vice-moderator of the preparatory group. It sets out the mandate of the preparatory group which is, in essence, to plan the programme and organize the world convocation theologically and administratively.

June 1988: First meeting of preparatory group at Crêt Bérard, Switzerland. It sets out the basic programme of the convocation, the possible venue, size and participation, and the outline of the document on theological affirmations on justice, peace and the integrity of creation. A decision is made to use the worship and plenary presentations at the convocation to present the reality of suffering and hope which JPIC is meant to address. These are to complement and stimulate the more rigorous intellectual work on the theological affirmation. The seven days of the meeting are to follow a liturgical sequence: Day 1: Praise and adoration. Day 2: Repentance/confession and announcing of forgiveness. Day 3: Proclamation of the word of hope. Day 4: Affirmation of faith. Day 5: Intercession. Day 6: Commitment. Day 7: Covenanting and sending forth. These roughly follow the high points of the covenant renewal ceremony as found in passages of the Old Testament, and are intended to bracket together the whole work of the convocation and its important themes, and to provide a sense of movement from the first to the last day.

July 1988: The WCC central committee accepts the proposals from the preparatory group with regard to programme, size of the convocation (550 persons) and the outline of the theological document.

September 1988: The Pacific Conference of Churches has a JPIC assembly in Malua, Apia, with the theme, "Renewing Our Partnership in God's Creation".

November 1988: A small group meets with WCC-JPIC staff in Montreux, Switzerland, to prepare a working draft of the theological affirmations for the convocation. The draft is sent in January 1989 to some 250 selected persons for their comments and criticisms.

February 1989: The Roman Catholic Church makes "A Catholic Contribution to the Process of Justice, Peace and the Integrity of Creation".

April 1989: The second meeting of the preparatory group in Baar, Switzerland. It uses the working draft and the responses to it to write the first draft, "Towards an Ecumenical Theological Affirmation on Justice, Peace and the Integrity of Creation". The first draft is sent in June 1989 to churches, movements, and all organizations wishing to participate in the convocation, with the request that responses to the draft be sent to the WCC-JPIC office by October 1989. (Though the time was short, more than 250 responses to the document were received.)

May 1989: Inter-Orthodox consultation on justice and peace meets in Minsk, Belorussia (USSR), and issues the document, "Orthodox Perspectives on Justice and Peace".

May 1989: The Conference of European Churches and the Council of European Bishops' Conferences (CCEE) jointly convene the European assembly on "Peace with Justice for the Whole Creation" in Basel, Switzerland. Around 700 delegates from churches and 900 others (including press) attend the assembly. The first major meeting of Catholic, Orthodox and Protestant churches since the great schism. The document of the assembly is accepted by an overwhelming majority (95.4 percent) and sent to the churches for study and action.

August 1989: The assembly of the World Alliance of Reformed Churches meeting in Seoul, Korea, has justice, peace and the integrity of creation as the theme of one of its sections. The report is in the form of an open letter to the younger generation which "inherits" the world of injustice, unpeace and environmental degradation that we have produced.

September 1989: The Christian Conference of Asia has a mission conference in Cipenas, Indonesia. With the theme "The Mission of God in the Context of Suffering and Struggling People in Asia", later changed to "Peoples of God, People of God", the conference discusses the implications of JPIC for Asia and Asian churches.

November 1989: An executive group from the preparatory group meets to issue the second draft of the preparatory document. This is sent out in December 1989 as the basic study document for the convocation.

December 1989: The Latin American Council of Churches (CLAI) convenes a meeting in Quito, Ecuador, on justice, peace and the integrity of creation using "land" and the "international debt crisis" as foci for discussing the importance of JPIC for Latin America.

January 1990: Last meeting of the preparatory group. It finalizes arrangements, working groups and drafting groups for the convocation. At this meeting, the preparatory group receives with shock the news, already communicated to the WCC general secretary on 18 November 1989 by the presidents of the Pontifical Councils for Promoting Christian Unity and for Justice and Peace, that the Roman Catholic Church will not officially participate in the convocation but will send twenty "experts" as observers.

February 1990: The assembly of the Lutheran World Federation meets in Curitiba, Brazil, and uses JPIC as a framework for the discussion of its theme, "I have heard the cry of my people".

5-12 March 1990: The world convocation on "Justice, Peace and the Integrity of Creation" meets in Seoul, Republic of Korea. Nearly one thousand people including visitors attend. The convocation issues a set of ten faith-affirmations and four "concretizations" of a covenant on justice, peace and the integrity of creation. Responses to the convocation are mixed and interpretations of its ecumenical significance vary from "the chaos that was Seoul" to "the ecumenical breakthrough at Seoul".

March 1990: The WCC central committee, meeting ten days after the convocation, receives a preliminary draft of the Seoul document and commends it to the churches for study and action. It reaffirms the long-term commitment of the WCC to JPIC and asks that JPIC be given a prominent place in the forthcoming assembly of the WCC. The Unit II report to the central committee speaks of JPIC as "at the heart of an ecumenical vision for the next millennium".

February 1991: The seventh assembly of the World Council of Churches meeting in Canberra, Australia, reflects the concerns of JPIC in all of its section reports on the theme "Come, Holy Spirit — Renew the Whole Creation!" The official reports of the assembly urge the continuance of JPIC in the work of the WCC.

August 1991: The assembly of the Caribbean Conference of Churches meets in Port of Spain, Trinidad, and deals with JPIC under the theme, "Participants in God's World — Preserve, Renew, Recreate".

September 1991: The WCC central committee creates a new Unit III, Justice, Peace and Creation: "the four areas of covenant on justice, peace, creation and racism... should be foundational for its programmatic work".

The Process Leading to Seoul and Canberra

Points of Strength and Weakness

Margot Kässmann

The time between the WCC assemblies in Vancouver 1983 and in Canberra 1991 was characterized by the struggle for JPIC — a struggle over the issues of JPIC as well as over the JPIC process. For those involved in the ecumenical movement it was a time of deep engagement. It was a time of hope and despair, of applause as well as criticism. Since I see every experience as a learning process for new tasks, in this personal reflection I would like to describe and interpret some of the difficulties during those years as steps forward.

Learning process

Much has been said about the deficiencies of the process. Summarizing these here again, I hope, will open the way for change, because in whatever form JPIC will be carried on after Canberra, these deficiencies could be avoided right from the beginning.

Co-ordination: The richness of the process for justice, peace and the integrity of creation revealed itself especially wherever JPIC began to be actualized locally. Many grassroot groups took up the idea and connected the theme they were working on with other themes and other groups. In that way, whole networks of groups and initiatives came into existence, and these live, work and grow even today. One of the problems was that there was no organized communication between the different networks. Geneva would have been the ideal place to start such co-ordination. For that the co-operation of the whole house would have been necessary. A concept such as JPIC cannot be treated as one among many on the ecumenical agenda. Many groups and networks which worked with enthusiasm and effectively on the local level looked desperately for contact with the wider process; they wanted something more than an address in a brochure. In particular, the interconnectedness of the issues — for many what was unique about the process — had to be proved and elaborated by scientific studies. This help was not available. One could hold forth on the connection between the debt crisis, the arms trade and the destruction of the tropical rain forest, but there was no systematic study to rely on. Thus many groups felt deserted by those who had started the process. They could not make the connections between the issues and the groups struggling with the issues.

Commitment: Commitment was to be the pillar of the process. But this was not reflected in any way in the concerns of the ecumenical movement. Soon there were protests: "Who or what is the WCC to give binding recommendations to the churches?" The whole ecclesiological debate in the ecumenical movement came to the fore. Again and again the Toronto Statement of 1950 was quoted; and time and again people questioned the use of the term "conciliar" in connection with ethical questions. More about that later. Here I just want to note that we cannot meaningfully talk about commitment when those who want to commit themselves are not ready to be committed.

Worldwide engagement: At the beginning the conciliar process was a Europe-centred, if not a German-centred, initiative. This created quite a problem. First of all, whether for reasons of lack of communication or suspicion, it took a long time for other regions to take up this initiative. Even when this happened, the efforts were not synchronized. If one region comes up with an initiative such as JPIC and wants it to have a worldwide impact, it must consult well in advance with the other regions in order to find out whether they will support it. Otherwise the initiative will never be truly owned by the whole ecumenical movement, and it will be suspect, as was clearly evident at the Seoul JPIC convocation. What made this part of the preparation more problematic was the way in which the conciliar process was mixed up with Carl Friedrich von Weizsäcker's initiative for a council for peace. He had in 1985 suggested that such a council, in the traditional meaning of the early church, should come together from 1987 to 1989 and during those two years carry out its task. The 1985 WCC central committee meeting in Buenos Aires tried to define the relationship between the two, but that definition, seeing the council for peace as a regional initiative within the conciliar process, was never really accepted. So the expectation of results was based on very different presuppositions. On the other hand, for many Europeans the European Ecumenical Assembly in Basel 1989 set the measure for the world convocation in Seoul 1990. They just could not see that they were dealing with two different enterprises. Among the differences were the defined aims of the two gatherings; the limited perception of one — and especially one very rich — continent; the nature of participation of the Roman Catholic Church; and different methodologies. So everyone who expected at Seoul a Basel meeting at a world level was disappointed. That this would not be the case should have been clear from the very beginning.

Preparation: Another problem was in the working of the preparatory group. Between the first meeting in Glion in 1986 and the next meeting in Geneva in 1987 there was almost a complete change of membership. After that, the group had only four opportunities to meet. And finally, the competences of the different members, the staff and other individuals, who were from time to time drawn into the process, were never quite clear. It was not clearly defined who was responsible for drafting, who for worship, who for programme. This caused unnecessary problems which could have been avoided through clarification right from the beginning. Nevertheless, the group finally grew together, in itself a deeply inspiring process.

The time-span given for preparing a world convocation on the main problems of the world was just impossible, considering the personnel and money made available. This should have been seen realistically. Indeed there was a suggestion to postpone the event, but nobody quite dared to.

Theology: Finally, the process leading to Seoul made it clear that the theological foundation of the JPIC process should have been tested thoroughly. I still believe that the concept of covenanting is a great achievement of the conciliar process. It was in the second draft of the preparatory document that it was dealt with in a way that we could work with. For those drafting, it was a great moment when we realized that all of us, whether Roman Catholic, Orthodox, Protestant or Anglican, whether African, European or Asian, could work with it because it is a biblical term. This could not however be conveyed to the delegates of the Seoul convocation and to the member churches. There were no real theological debates on the concept, only some minor arguments. Faith and Order and its commission had been asked several times to help with clarifications, a request repeated at the March 1990 central committee.

But this request was not picked up, perhaps because Faith and Order does not see its task as providing the theological bases for programmes of the Council. The JPIC office and preparatory group on the other hand were not equipped to provide that help.

Crisis as progress

The process leading to Seoul and Canberra was more than a learning process. My thesis is that many of the deficiencies point to a deep crisis in the ecumenical movement itself. To see the difficulties in such a way would pave the way for a successful JPIC process in the future. By bringing the conflicts and the problems into the open there could be a breakthrough, even though for many of those involved this was and is at times hard to accept.

Regional preparation: Because of the Europe-centred beginning of the JPIC process there was a lack of preparation in the other regions for the world convocation in Seoul. So in a way the preparatory document took the second step before the first: it talked about the worldwide dimension of injustice, war and the destruction of creation before clarifying the specific regional aspects. Thus many delegates had the feeling that their region and their problems did not get enough attention in Seoul. This points to a wider problem in the World Council: how can you talk at a general level when people are suspicious that it might exclude the specifics of their own contexts? How can you come together from several different contextual approaches? We have in the last years learned how valuable and enriching the contextual approach is. Now we have to ask what it would mean to go forward together, from contextual to ecumenical theology, if such a step is possible.

Relations with the Roman Catholic Church: Already at the 1985 central committee meeting, it was felt that the conciliar process for JPIC should not take place without the participation of the Roman Catholic Church. At the following central committee in January 1987 an official invitation was sent to the Vatican. That should have been done much earlier. As it happened, the WCC waited until December 1987 for an answer, and could not really start working because of the fear that the RCC might feel excluded. It meant 1987 too was a lost year; 1983 to 1985 had already been lost because of changes in the leadership of the Council. When the Vatican finally answered, the form of participation it was proposing was quite unclear. It was said that there would be responsible though not equal sharing in staff involvement and preparation, though it never quite worked out. In fact the WCC tried various things and drafted documents all of which the Vatican criticized without really having had any responsibility in the process of initiating or preparing them. This also caused much tension within the preparatory group. It reached its peak during the meeting of January 1990 at which the members of the preparatory group sent by the Vatican were present even though the Vatican had said (a few days after we had finished the second draft document with the participation of people sent by the Vatican!) that it would not send delegates but only a few advisers to Seoul.

During all this, there was a lack of reliable arrangements. For instance, it was assumed that the Vatican would send fifty delegates to Seoul, but there was no written agreement to that effect signed by anybody responsible in Rome. Both the WCC and its member churches did not seem to know what they were doing. Often the WCC looked like an abandoned lover running after his girl despite all the hurt and pain she was giving him. This whole issue is not only a JPIC-connected question. The WCC and the member churches must clarify their relationship with the Roman Catholic Church and take a clear stand. Otherwise they will not be taken seriously by the RCC which will also underestimate their significance.

This section would be incomplete if we did not mention that at the same time there was a deeply inspiring and enriching process of co-operation with Roman Catholic Christians at the level of groups, parishes and regions. Many felt this as a contradiction — that while there was co-operation at the local level this experience could not be reflected at the world level; and that in face of the most challenging questions of our days the churches could not work together.

Relations between groups and churches: One of the main points of debate with the Vatican was, time and again, the participation of groups defined as a number of Christians coming together at local or regional levels to work for justice, peace and the integrity of creation. These groups have in the last several years been a source of inspiration for the churches in the area of social-ethical issues. Therefore they were supposed to play a significant role in the conciliar process and in the convocation at Seoul. The churches were asked to send members of such groups or grassroot initiatives as part of their delegations. About thirty percent of the participants in Seoul were to be of that category. Yet, repeatedly their status and competence were questioned. As a consequence the delegates from the grassroots organizations did not see the convocation as their own, and tended to give the impression that by fighting the concept of the convocation they were fighting the establishment of the churches. This too is not simply a problem of the world convocation but of the WCC and its member churches.

While some sub-units such as the Commission on the Churches' Participation in Development (CCPD) work closely with such groups, other sub-units ignore them altogether. While some member churches live in close relationship with those groups, others do not know how to relate to them.

Ecclesiology: The relationship between movements and churches is part of a greater ecclesiological problem that the conciliar process again brought into the open.

First of all, the member churches of the WCC have insisted since 1950 that the WCC has no authority to give them binding advice on their internal affairs. Thus, there is no commitment, and they feel no obligation to follow the recommendations of the World Council meetings. The idea of the conciliar process was that through it there would be a reliable and co-ordinated process of speaking and acting on the part of the churches on burning social, ethical and political issues, and in fact this commitment should be part of the definition of what it is to be the church. This thrust was resisted again and again by questioning the use of the term "conciliar" in connection with issues of justice, peace and the integrity of creation. Similarly, the term "covenant" was also questioned. Here too there is a conflict that the WCC and its member churches must solve: can you talk about the unity of the church without relating it to the divisions in the world caused by injustice, war and destruction? The old conflict between Faith and Order and Life and Work is once again evident here.

Communication within the WCC: JPIC was supposed to be an overall concern of the WCC. That is, all sub-units and units would have to relate their work to it and strengthen it through co-operation among themselves. To be fair, it needs to be said that some sub-units tried to co-operate but others for the most part went about their business because they had enough on their own agenda. In recent years there has been much discussion about restructuring the WCC. It has been said several times that for reasons of clarity, of perception and of effectiveness programmes have to be better co-ordinated. The JPIC process could have been an example of such co-ordination.

Participation and methodology: Finally there is a methodological problem, evident at most of the WCC meetings during the last few years, that was also present at Seoul.

— How can people who concentrate on paper and those who concentrate on experience, those who expect resolutions and those who expect action to produce a particular result, work together?
— How do old-timers and new-comers get into real dialogue, and how do we learn to listen to one another?
— How do we effectively bring together group reports and plenary reports? (In Seoul people felt that they could not find what they had said in their group report in the composite report that was presented at the plenary. Some who had not been successful in having an amendment accepted in their group could get it through at the plenary.)
— How do we transfer what happens in conferences to the churches at home?
— How do we stop the destructive way of fighting for hours over minor changes and thereby not having time for a real debate on the issue itself?
— How do we prepare well enough in the regions and then bring the regional results together at the meeting?
— How do we bring the worship life of a meeting into a creative relationship with the rest of what is taking place?

As long as there are no new ideas on how to handle these problems there should be a moratorium on world conferences because right now they are not all that effective.

Finally, a main methodological problem not directly connected with conferences is how to move from reflection to action. There were suggestions all over the world during the process about how to translate JPIC into practice, but there seemed to be a very wide range of possibilities. The discussion about starting by restricting action to one issue in order to be heard and seen was problematic because there was hardly any agreement on a crucial issue with which to begin. The four areas that were finally suggested at the convocation were then interpreted so widely that no less than 86 proposals for action emerged. Certainly, action on the debt crisis will look very differently in different regions, but 86 is far too many and one does not know even where to start. And then there is the question of accountability. The suggestion that came up in the preparatory group to send, after two years, a team to visit the member churches in order to monitor progress was defeated. Again, the appeal was to the autonomy of member churches in which the WCC had no right to interfere.

My hope is that by studying these problems of the WCC and its member churches which became apparent in the conciliar process, there will be an opportunity to take a step forward.

Between Seoul and Canberra

The central committee meeting in March 1990 gave much time to a discussion on the impact of Seoul and the future of JPIC. For the first time there was a feeling that this committee owned the process, that the regional and ecclesiological problems could be overcome because this process is of crucial importance to all member churches. The committee unanimously voted for a text and the far-reaching recommendations for the future of JPIC. For many involved this was a remarkable moment because it seemed that finally, after all the difficulties, JPIC was making its impact.

When the preparatory group met again in May 1990 in order to evaluate the world convocation and to ask how it could transmit it to the member churches and to the WCC assembly in Canberra, it found out that the meeting itself should not have taken place! Its work was supposed to be over with Seoul, and there was no money left. That meant not only that the group would not be able to produce a proper documentation of the Seoul conference, but also that it would not be able to prepare the plenary and the worship planned for Canberra. So Marga Bührig, one of the moderators of the preparatory group, wrote in the name of all members a letter to the general secretary of the World Council of Churches insisting that the decisions of the 1990 central committee meeting be honoured and stressing the need for a "centre of exchange":

> It took three years following the Vancouver assembly to achieve a functioning staff unit. The JPIC process could not sustain a further interruption of that kind after Canberra. Continuity is required to support the process and service the member churches. While JPIC is a Council-wide programme, the issues with which it is dealing suggest that Unit II is the appropriate location for the JPIC's "centre of exchange, information and challenge", at least as an interim arrangement until decisions regarding a more permanent solution have been made.

Most of the JPIC staff left, the preparatory group could not meet again, and a staff task force prepared the JPIC events for Canberra. There was a plenary with three good speeches. But there were two deficiencies. First, it did not manage to point to the war in the Persian Gulf as an example of the interconnectedness of justice, peace and the integrity of creation. This would have had a great impact and helped new delegates to understand what JPIC is all about. Second, the plenary did not allow room to discuss the challenge to the churches and the WCC to continue this process, and to take the commitment from Seoul as their own. Thus, JPIC was just one plenary among others and was not owned by the delegates and, therefore, by the member churches.

The adviser for JPIC at Canberra and several delegations tried again very hard to get the "centre of exchange" going right after Canberra, but the programme policy committee rejected these concrete proposals for financial reasons as well as for reasons of restructuring the programme of the WCC. So, hope for the future of JPIC now lies in the proposal of the Programme Policy Committee report that JPIC is the perspective from which the WCC in future should handle social-ethical challenges. We hope that in the restructuring this emphasis will give JPIC a prominent place in the work of the council. The worldwide JPIC process will continue to demand a prominent place for JPIC in the Council; and those who know the history of a "just, participatory and sustainable society" (JPSS) know what damage can be done by creating new programmes in the place of old ones which have begun to make an impact.

The World Convocation

Problems, Achievements

Marga Bührig

Unity as worldwide consensus

Even before the world convocation was over some smart journalists had decided it was a failure. It was not to be compared with the European assembly (Basel, May 1989) on the same themes. It was not the hoped-for "council" at which Christians of all confessions, or rather all the Christian churches together, were to have spoken with one voice on urgent world problems in such a way that the world would have had to listen.

True, it was none of those things. But the question is whether the expectations were not too high ever to be fulfilled and the standards set inappropriate for a such a convocation. Or, to put it more clearly: it was wrong to take a successful European example (Basel) as the model for a world gathering and expect more or less the same thing to happen in a wider framework. That was to underestimate the much more complex dynamics of a world meeting and to fail to appreciate the sharpness of the North-South conflict and all the enemy images and emotions that go with it.

Apart from that, at a time when there are deep divisions within individual churches (e.g. between fundamentalism and liberation theology in any form) and, conversely, common elements cutting across all confessional boundaries (e.g. experiences in various kinds of grassroots

---

• This text, written in the first half of 1991, was translated from the German by the WCC Language Service.

communities), it is questionable whether we can still seek unity in the sense of worldwide consensus. A good example of this was the draft preparatory document "Between the Flood and the Rainbow". This had been prepared by a committee whose members came from the different continents and church traditions, but it was vehemently criticized as one-sidedly European. Africans, Latin Americans and Asians did not recognize their own situation in what it said. In the preparatory committee we had debated whether or not to present concrete examples by name and had in most cases decided not to do so — or at least not to name specific situations. We tried instead to start with the global threats to life and move on from there to theological statements. As a result, we were criticized by many Europeans who said the analysis was too superficial and the theology not comprehensive enough because it had not taken in all the fullness of the biblical message.

The non-Europeans, on the other hand, looked in vain for their particular concrete problems and concerns. For me it is debatable whether we can today produce truly "ecumenical" documents which go beyond a few undisputed basic affirmations of the biblical faith. Against this background it is nothing short of a miracle that we were still able to enter into acts of covenanting at Seoul. These, too, are not concerned with abstract dogmatics, but with the commitment to solidarity on certain specific issues, from the starting point of our own respective situations and always set in the perspective of God's love for the world.

Confirmation of our covenant with God and with one another

When I try to assess for myself the real results of the world convocation, I think immediately of the four acts of covenanting and the ten affirmations that accompany them. There have been endless debates on whether the word "covenant" is appropriate here. The biblical term means that God has established a covenant with us human beings — from the covenant with Noah, Abraham and the people of Israel to the "new" covenant in Jesus Christ; but that we human beings as partners of this covenant are constantly departing from it and violating it. In ancient Israel there were rituals for the renewal of the covenant on the human side. Heino Falcke, in an article in *The Ecumenical Review*, outlines the stages of this renewal: remembering that from God's side this covenant is firm and unshakeable, proclamation of God's will for his people, renouncing false gods, celebration of the covenant or its renewal, and the opening up of the covenant. The intention is not exclusive but inclusive. Our own act of covenanting was a bold step to see our commitment to work for justice, peace and the integrity of creation as the renewal and confirmation of our covenant with God and with one another. In the message of the world convocation we read:

> Now is the time to commit ourselves anew to God's covenant. The moment of history is unique. All life on earth is threatened by injustice, war and destruction because we have turned away from God's covenant...
>
> Now is the time to consolidate all struggles for justice, peace and the integrity of creation. We must free ourselves from bondage to power structures which blind us and make us accomplices in destruction. Christians have to move out into the world to which Jesus came.
>
> Now is the time for the ecumenical movement to articulate its vision of all people living on earth and caring for creation as a family... This vision... must be expressed in concrete action. On the basis of our spiritual experience here in Seoul we have committed ourselves to work for:
> — a just economic order and for liberation from the foreign debt bondage;
> — the true security of all nations and people and for a culture of non-violence;
> — building a culture that can live in harmony with creation's integrity and for preserving the gift of the earth's atmosphere;
> — the eradication of racism and discrimination on all levels for all people, and for the dismantling of patterns of behaviour that perpetuate the sin of racism.

It may be thought that we had taken a lot upon ourselves, and a detailed reading of the full texts only enhances this impression. For reasons of time it was not possible in Seoul to discuss the many facets of these acts of covenanting. We discussed only the main lines and adopted the acts of covenanting as a whole almost unanimously. The big question is, what do we do with them now? In accepting them, those who voted for them, and the many who could not vote but nevertheless agreed entirely with them in spirit, also undertook to take these commitments back with them to their churches or groups and to continue working on them in one way or another. We who were present have committed ourselves together before God and before one another, and we are mutually accountable.

Most of us had been involved in these issues and discussions before Seoul. Has the act of covenanting, reaffirmed in the worship service, done anything to enhance this? Or will it end up as a theological superstructure to hide our actual powerlessness and helplessness?

Only a few days after the world convocation, the central committee of the World Council of Churches meeting in Geneva took note of the findings of the Seoul convocation and recommended them for further consideration at the forthcoming assembly at Canberra in February 1991.

On the edge of this meeting I had a conversation with a German bishop who is well disposed towards the concerns of the world convocation. But he was against the use of the term "covenant"; he could not understand how this term had come to be chosen nor what made this act of covenanting any different from any other declaration of intention. It was difficult to explain clearly to him what we had meant and what the Seoul documents actually stated. It was and is a question of fulfilling the mandate of the assembly in Vancouver in 1983 which proposed that the WCC "call the member churches to engage... in a conciliar process of mutual commitment (covenant) to justice, peace and the integrity of creation". The covenant is more than just a plain agreement that has been given theological trappings.

The question is, are we capable of understanding and accepting it as a basis for our lives and how far is it possible to carry that over into our churches? There is considerable difference between the public debate now going on everywhere on factual subjects such as the greenhouse effect, and the deep, serious commitment to the God who is not obliged to renew his covenant with us. One of the major concerns of the world convocation was to hold the two in tension. The bridge between faith and "political" commitment was the daily worship service which followed a pattern based on praise and adoration, penitence and confession, proclamation of the word of hope, affirmation of faith, intercession, covenanting and mission, but which also related directly to the content of the commitments.

Now everything is different: "We are in covenant"

The fact that covenanting really had changed something was brought home to me most clearly by the words of a Korean participant on the day after the world convocation ended. He had already been deeply involved in the preparatory work. He said: "Now everything is different: we are in covenant."

We have here ten affirmations which were adopted by an overwhelming majority after lengthy and sometimes difficult discussions. They are an essential part of the covenant — indeed, someone has called them the foundations of a socio-ethical catechism. The themes as included in the message of the conference are:
— all exercise of power is accountable to God;
— God's option for the poor;
— the equal value of all races and peoples;
— male and female are created in the image of God;

— truth is at the foundation of a community of free people;
— the peace of Jesus Christ;
— the creation as beloved of God;
— the earth is the Lord's;
— the dignity and commitment of the younger generation;
— human rights are given by God.

Here, too, people may say: "We have heard that many times before." But I believe there is truth in what one Swiss journalist wrote: these affirmations are highly explosive and they will be worth a closer examination when they appear in print. What would be the consequences if our churches took seriously the affirmation that all exercise of power is accountable to God — including the power of rich church bureaucracies? What would be the consequences if this gave them a new authority to intervene in favour of the full participation of everyone in decision-making processes in the world of work and political life? It sounds so harmless to say: "The earth is the Lord's." But if this affirmation of faith is made in our own life situation, then our church communities will have to look responsibly at how they treat the precious land, and on which side they stand when it comes to real estate speculation or the desecration of the countryside and pollution of our air and water.

These themes bring us to the act of covenanting for an economic order centred on human beings and not on profit and, at the same time, make us aware of our own powerlessness. We realize how much easier it is to formulate statements like this than to put even one small part of them into practice. The great danger is that everything may simply remain on paper. If this happens, then Seoul is a failure.

The ten affirmations are all formulated in the same way: the theme is stated and then they go on to say: "we affirm... we resist... we commit..." For example:

> We affirm that access to truth and education, information and means of communication are basic human rights...
> We resist policies that deny freedom of expression; that encourage the concentration of the communication media in the hands of the state or economically powerful monopolies...
> We commit ourselves to create means by which the neglected and vulnerable may learn and the silenced may make themselves heard...

The rhythm recurring in each of these affirmations might make it possible for congregations or action groups to build them into worship and so render the step from statement of faith to resistance and commitment easier to understand. It should be made clear that the individual texts in each case can of course be altered. The Seoul texts are not dogma, but these are subjects that have emerged out of long ecumenical discussion and they do deserve to be taken seriously and tested in different situations.

The threats are inter-related

It was a deliberate decision on my part to begin this article with the findings of the meeting before reporting on how they came about. There were about a thousand men and women in Seoul: some four hundred voting delegates from the member churches of the WCC, sixty advisers, and forty official guests. The others were journalists and visitors. Delegates from the third world, really the two-thirds world, were in the majority and this strongly influenced the overall work of the convocation. In the preparatory work we had tried to show the inherent relationship of justice, peace and the integrity of creation, or to put it the other way round, how injustice, violence and the destruction of creation are inter-linked and interwoven. In the draft document we read: "But what is most significant in all this — and what is grasped by too few people! — is that none of these threats can be combated effectively if they are isolated from one another. The real danger lies in the fact that they are inseparably linked, and that it requires both knowledge and wisdom to imaginatively discern this linkage. In a society that rewards specializations and discourages holistic learning, such wisdom is rare! From now on, it must be consciously pursued and nurtured."

Was this view generally accepted? In Seoul delegates from Africa and Latin America emphasized strongly, even heatedly, that for them the question of justice was central, i.e. it has to precede even the elimination of poverty (debt crisis, hunger) or eradication of racism in all its forms. Those of us from the rich industrialized countries had to heed this message and it challenged our tendency to concern ourselves first and foremost with the integrity of creation and the preservation of the earth's atmosphere. Of course we have good reason for seeing the latter as our most urgent task. But I hope it has been brought home to us afresh just how big and how unjust is the imbalance that exists between North and South and that in everything we do or do not do, we have to take account of the situation of the "others". We cannot, for instance, ban the use of certain pesticides or medicines in our part of the world and export them thoughtlessly to others. "We cannot do that...", and yet we do! But here, too, the blame cannot be apportioned to one side alone, for the interlinking of the world economy is such that it has partners in the two-thirds world; and in our countries, too, there are people who suffer and are oppressed. Nonetheless the heavier burden lies with the North. Seoul left us in no doubt about that.

The voice of the others came to us in another way at two worship services, when we heard men and women giving testimonies of both suffering and hope. We heard of suffering, for instance, through the voice of a young woman representing the Aboriginal people of Australia who told us what had happened to her people during the two hundred years of white rule. We heard the unforgettable testimony of a Japanese woman living and working with Filippino women driven by poverty to work in Japanese pleasure houses and brothels. She spoke in the first person, representing the many women whose first name is always "baby", the next name "dancer", "stripper", "prostitute" — and whose last name is "AIDS". Testimonies to hope came, for example, from a student in the former German Democratic Republic and a Christian from the United States living with the poorest of the poor in the slums of Washington; they gave us vivid descriptions of the situations in their own countries but they also told us of faith and hope:

> The historic events we witness today are prophetic. Today it is an east wind of freedom and democracy that is blowing out the old. Tomorrow it will be a south wind of justice and liberation to set free the oppressed... It's hard to stop the wind when it begins to blow.

Lastly, especially in the worship services, we experienced at first hand the richness of the different forms of expression of the Christian faith in music, Bible study, images and movement. This life of worship was an important ingredient in the spiritual basis from which the acts of covenanting, the affirmations and the commitments could grow.

Women at the world convocation

Women were fairly well represented at all levels of the meeting and in all offices. The numerical balance of men to women was five to three. A Swiss Roman Catholic who was present in Seoul as a journalist described the effect of the women's presence as follows:

> The great gain at Seoul was the emergence of a new manner of discussion to which the women made a decisive contribution. The women's forum used dramatic presentations to demonstrate the idea that women in this process are not just objects to be discussed, but active subjects. This changed the style for everyone, men and women. This freedom of speech is perhaps the decisive

human right which gives all the acts of covenanting at the world convocation in Seoul their special character.

This freedom of speech was accorded and used. Nevertheless, it did not prove possible to enable women, and also young people, to contribute their very specific experiences as penetratingly as had been intended. They were often referred to passively in the phrase "especially women and children". On international Women's Day, women also covenanted with one another, but it was possible only to a limited extent to include their demands as an integral part at all stages. Nonetheless, in my view, Seoul also marked a step forward in this respect.

How much authority do the churches still have?

Despite all the difficulties (visas, accommodation, distance) Seoul proved a good choice. We were confronted every day with the very themes we were discussing: a huge city of some ten million inhabitants, with an "Olympic Park" of almost incredible proportions built on the rubble of the bulldozed huts of the poor. On every side the influence of international consumer economies growing, indifferent to the real needs of people. Korea is still divided into North and South, not of its own volition but by the manoeuvring super-powers. The border at the 38th parallel is said to be the most heavily armed frontier in the world, with the biggest number of nuclear weapons. It divides around ten million people from family and friends living on either side of it. Any attempt to cross this border is punished, even in the "democratic" South. Reunification is a subject that sets many hearts on fire. A high point of the convocation was the "Korean evening" organized for us by our hosts, the Korean Council of Churches. It included a presentation in dance, images and words of Korea's heart-breaking history and its hope of reunification. Korean Christians have declared the year 1995 as a "Year of Jubilee" and hope then, fifty years after the end of the Japanese occupation, to be able to celebrate reunification. In its message, the world convocation expressed solidarity with this aim.

This brings us back once again to the question: what does all this mean? And the other question: is this really a task for Christian churches and individuals? For the Korean Christians who were with us it meant the assurance that they have the support of a worldwide community of faith in dealing with one of their very specific problems. Delegates from Sweden, Switzerland, Poland and Czechoslovakia took a practical step. Soldiers from these four countries are stationed on the border at the 38th parallel, and are silently present at the ritual of the official "talks" between North and South Korea. Now the representatives of the churches in these countries have "covenanted". They plan to meet again in August 1991 and discuss whether there are steps towards understanding that they and their governments could take.

Referring to a report on Seoul in a Basel newspaper, a critical participant asked me whether "Seoul" had not got through to the politicians. I was at a loss to answer that particular question. But I do not think that was the aim of the meeting. The world convocation was a process of awareness-building among the churches and Christian people, and an act of faith. What was special about it was that it took up themes of great political relevance. How much weight and authority do the churches still have? That is a question which cannot be answered in general terms. In the GDR, for example, we saw Christians and churches playing a major role in the whole uprising. Much will depend on how the churches participating in the process deal with what happened in Seoul. The member churches of the World Council of Churches were challenged again at their assembly in Canberra in February 1991. I see it as a hopeful sign that among the visitors at Seoul there were so many people representing active groups working on the fringe of the church, including many from the Roman Catholic Church which sent only a small official delegation. All of these people belong in the "covenant", they are part of the conciliar process and we who were in Seoul hope that many other brothers and sisters will join us. That is the only way to reach a wider public.

The People of God and the Conciliar Process

Marc Reuver

The years between the World Council of Churches' assemblies in Vancouver (1983) and Canberra (1991) are marked by events that profoundly touched the fate of the human family. The decades-old Cold War between East and West disappeared and the socialist Marxist-Stalinist state system broke down. The nuclear threat diminished, but the institutionalized injustice which enables the Western and Northern economic power elites to colonialize and exploit the developing countries in the South remained unchanged. The Gulf war was probably a desperate attempt along this line. During the same period the emerging peoples all over the world in various ways resisted the ruthless oppression they had suffered through centuries and tried to take their destiny into their own hands.

It is against this background that the Vancouver decision to call the Christian world to a commitment to justice, peace and the integrity of creation and the conciliar process which resulted from this call should be assessed.

The conciliar process had a difficult start. It was an ambitious task entrusted to the central committee of the World Council and the WCC staff. It was associated with the ideal of growing into a peace council as formulated by the German professor von Weizsäcker. But a peace council would have to include the participation of the Roman Catholic Church. However, Rome as well as the Orthodox churches had a different idea of the theological and ecclesiological meaning of a council. The result of the debates on the concept and meaning of a council was that the conciliar process from the start was almost exclusively identified with the church hierarchies and church officials.

The WCC central committee meeting in 1985 rejected the idea of calling together a global peace council. Instead the proposal now was to convene a world convocation which would produce authoritative declarations from church officials who would commit themselves and their institutions to decisive actions and mutual covenants. This new direction suffered from an almost endless debate on how far the Roman Catholic Church would participate in the preparations for the world convocation and in the actual drawing up of its official documents.

While discussions on the nature and the status of the world convocation went on among members of the central committee and the church officials the conciliar process unexpectedly developed its own character. The Christian world, the people of God in its manifold expressions of action groups, peace movements, grassroots communities and the like, interpreted the call for justice, peace and the integrity of creation according to their own existential needs. The Vancouver call became for the poor, the exploited and the suffering a very strong instrument in their struggle for survival against the forces of death. It meant for Christians all over the world a sign of hope and solidarity. The specific interpretation of the issues of justice, peace and the integrity of creation according to the peculiar local, national and regional needs ensured that the conciliar process became contextualized. While East German Christians used the conciliar process, often against the will of their church leaders, as a means to liberate themselves from the communist regime, the same process helped the Caribbeans in their struggle for the defence of human rights, and the Latin Americans to fight for their own land.

A variety of approaches — common elements

The JPIC progress report of 1988 underlined the ways of living out the various elements of the conciliar process and also brought to the fore the underlying common characteristics. The report listed the following major points:

1. Christians and churches worldwide are involved in the struggle against the forces of injustice and death. This action is taking various forms according to the context and the specific nature of the threats. In some countries it is explicitly and consciously related to the conciliar process, while in other places Christians are so concerned

with their daily struggle against oppressive and threatening situations that they do not have the time to make a conscious link with the conciliar process. In each case, however, the gospel message and the witness of Christians and Christian churches provide an alternative to the established order on the issues of justice, peace and the integrity of creation.

2. In Europe and North America, the previous concentration on nuclear issues is expanding to include studies on the interconnectedness between nuclear deterrence, global injustice including the international debt, unjust world economic systems, and the devastation of the natural environment. Moreover, the church institutions and the church-related action groups and organizations on these continents are prophetically speaking out on domestic issues such as racism, unemployment, social services and health care, the problems of "guest workers" and asylum-seekers, economic injustice and military budgets. They are pointing out how these domestic issues are global and inter-related.

3. In developing countries Christians play an important role in resisting oppression. Political and economic liberation is a central concern in these countries where the people have lived for so long under various forms of domination and oppression — racist, sexist, capitalist. Under the umbrella of the conciliar process Christians are consciously involved in the struggle for liberation. In this struggle they rediscover and are empowered by the liberating force of the gospel. This occurs most frequently among base Christian communities where the gospel is being re-read from the perspective of the poor and the oppressed and enacted in bold and fresh ways, in resistance and protest, in dance and celebration, in solidarity and hope. It is in this context that new contextual theologies are emerging.

4. The conciliar process is for many in different situations the appropriate means to fight for the defence of human rights. This goes in particular for the role and rights of women in church and society, which are, for the first time, being addressed throughout the Christian world. This is not happening without a struggle, however, for in many places discrimination against and abuse and oppression of women continue. The emergence of a "feminist theology", the presence of women in leadership roles in church, governments and industry and the growing awareness of the abuse and exploitation of women are opening doors towards the gospel vision that in Christ there is "neither male nor female" and that all are one in him.

5. The conciliar process has been a specific means of promoting the awareness that the struggle against the threats to life is a common ecumenical task. It calls for active collaboration with Roman Catholics. On the local level, even on the national and regional levels, the difficulties and hesitations shown by the Vatican to collaborate with the conciliar process are not shared. In many local congregations Roman Catholics have joined with Protestants, even with the encouragement of church leaders, to form JPIC ecumenical action groups. The collaboration on the ecumenical level is even more evident in the case of base communities where religious or denominational differences count little in the common everyday struggles of people. This is also true in affluent countries where ecumenical solidarity and collaboration transcend denominational lines as Christians and Christian organizations work together on issues of justice, peace and the integrity of creation.

The 1989 progress report concentrated on the many meetings, conferences and consultations which were held all over the world to coordinate the activities of the conciliar process and to prepare for the 1990 world convocation. In *Africa* the meetings concentrated on the extreme poverty of the people, the natural calamities, the burden of unbearable foreign debt, the increasing militarization of the continent and the violation of human rights. The need to understand theologically the peoples' struggles was one of the major issues. Five local seminars of women took place before a regional encounter on the response of women to the JPIC issues. In *Southern Africa* the struggle against apartheid was seen as a particular issue within the framework of the conciliar process.

From the Indian sub-continent came an appeal to the whole *Asian* population "that Christians and Christian churches should get involved in the struggles of the people against political, social and economic injustices". The Christian Conference of Asia took the lead in applying the conciliar process to the different situations of the Asian continent.

In the *Caribbean* the programme on "ecumenism and social change in obedience to Jesus Christ and in solidarity with the poor" was widely endorsed and implemented according to the specific local needs. Protestants and Roman Catholics worked closely together to apply this programme to local situations.

In *Europe* it was the Basel ecumenical assembly on "Peace and Justice" (15-21 May 1989) that made headlines. Representatives of Orthodox and Protestant churches, the Roman Catholic bishops' conferences, Christian peace movements, action groups, grassroots communities, women's associations and individual Christians experienced together an open engagement in the issues of justice, peace and the integrity of creation, their inter-relatedness and their impact on Europe and on relationships with the third world.

The *Latin American* Council of Churches (CLAI) convoked a continental conference during which the "contextualization" of the conciliar process emphasized three major issues: the importance of land, the negative impact of the external debt, and the necessity to fight for the defence of human rights.

The conciliar process in the *Middle East* was deeply concerned over the Israeli-Palestinian conflict which was seen as a permanent threat to peace not only for the region but also for the world as a whole.

In encounters in the *Pacific* the conciliar process was seen as providing strong support in the struggle against the militarization of the region, against the nuclear tests and the dumping of nuclear waste, and against the abuses of the tourist industry.

The Seoul world convocation

All these issues and problems, together with the specific input of the Orthodox churches, the World Alliance of Reformed Churches, the Lutheran World Federation and the historic Peace churches were presented at the world convocation in Seoul. The specific development of the conciliar process as traced in these pages came to the fore in Seoul and posed some problems. First of all the contextualization of the conciliar process, of the JPIC issues, and the very different contents given to the process by the national delegations, created a serious obstacle to a fruitful dialogue in Seoul. Furthermore, the great success of the European Basel meeting made the delegates from third-world countries, directly engaged in the struggles for life, even more afraid that the delegates from the rich countries would have the predominant voice. They felt powerless because of the absence of regional or continental consensus on mutual commitments and statements. Another difficulty was the relationship between churches, church-related social movements and non-church-related movements and groups. Many of these movements had challenged the churches concerning the JPIC issues in ways that made church leaders rather uncomfortable and even embarrassed. In an interview the WCC general secretary, Emilio Castro, clearly stated that many churches had difficulties with the role that movements had taken in the unfolding of the conciliar process. According to him the difficulties over Roman Catholic participation also arose out of this problem. Rome could not understand how the World Council of Churches could bring together official church representatives for issuing official statements and mutual commitments (covenants) and at the same time involve all kinds of Christian action groups. Rome as well as many Orthodox and Protestant church leaders refused to be identified with the specific areas of active involvement in the struggles for life as favoured by action groups. But in general, Seoul tried, and succeeded to an extent, in harmonizing the attitude of the official church representatives with the commitment of activists involved in people's struggles.

From Seoul to Canberra

The period following Seoul was, first of all, characterized by the very positive, even enthusiastic, response to the Seoul final document expressed by all kinds of action groups and base communities in many parts of the world. These groups saw the results of Seoul as supporting their daily and concrete struggles against the forces of injustice and death. The JPIC newsletter issued in Geneva wrote about the conciliar process as a movement owned by the people:

> It has been fascinating to observe how the commitment to justice, peace and the integrity of creation has left the churches and the documents, and is carried by the people. It is coming back to us now diversified and strengthened because it is applied to a concrete struggle in the different contexts. What is currently happening to JPIC is the aim of every programme that is launched — to become alive at the base and to inform the institutions.

In order to illustrate this process a reference to the Kairos movement may be relevant. Already at the Basel European event, "Kairos-Europe — Towards a Europe for Justice" was launched. The year 1992, which marks five hundred years of colonial power as well as the integration of the European Community internal market, could be viewed as the beginning of a new stage in the consolidation of economic power in Europe and the continuation of economic colonialization of Southern and Central America. The network Kairos-Europe was launched to address this new concentration of power in Europe and the growing oppression resulting from it. The Christian motivation of action groups initiating Kairos-Europe is the biblical perspective that amongst the poor we find God and that it is only through the poor that we shall find our liberation and build a just and peaceful society. The Greek word kairos stands both for a decisive time of judgment and an opportunity to strengthen the struggle for justice and capture a new vision of peace.

The Kairos-Europe idea was launched as a means to continue the conciliar process. It was meant for all groups and movements in Europe which had been active in one way or another in the conciliar process. Since the initiative was started, many alliances have been built among grassroots groups and movements to resist together poverty and marginalization which result from the European mechanisms of power. Many initiatives on the local, national and regional level have been taken.

For North America the Seoul convocation marked the beginning of a particular conciliar process. The US participants in Seoul founded "Kairos 1992 USA". The initiative focuses on the 1992 "celebration" of Columbus' arrival in the Americas. Within the framework of the conciliar process the initiative invites all church-related action groups and grassroots movements to reflect on the Columbus event. Actions are being organized against the symbols and realities of oppression that have resulted over the last five centuries since the so-called discovery of America by Columbus. Special attention is being given to the violence perpetrated against indigenous populations and the genocide of many native American tribes. The present situation of American indigenous people will be the centre of concern for Kairos 1992 USA. Instead of celebrating the fifth centenary, Kairos 1992 USA invites the American people to repent. The Kairos 1992 idea, which was started by lay people, is now receiving favourable response from several churches in the USA.

A similar "Kairos Latin America 1992" was launched from Seoul. Those who took the initiative stated that the commemoration of five hundred years of evangelization should recall the massacre of the indigenous people and the destruction of their cultures by the colonial powers, and also celebrate the centuries of resistance by the people. The aim of CLAI, which is one of the major organizations involved, is to support and promote initiatives and projects which attempt to recover Latin American history, and in particular to be of practical assistance to the indigenous peoples and their rehabilitation.

The various Kairos movements are in contact with one another and there are plans to organize a measure of global co-ordination.

While here we see a movement within the conciliar process, which developed almost exclusively at the grassroots level, the seventh assembly of the World Council of Churches which met in Canberra, Australia, 7-20 February 1991, was the occasion for the official church representatives to assess the conciliar process, amidst the strong presence and contribution of the Australian Aborigines. The assembly decided that the conciliar process should continue and that the three issues of justice, peace and the integrity of creation should constitute major thrusts for the ecumenical movement in the years ahead. The three issues provide an effective framework for witnessing to the justice of the kingdom of God and for resisting injustice, be it economic, political, cultural or social, of gender, race or ecology. The assembly recommended working towards a new theology of creation to enable the churches to play a meaningful role in the renewal of creation and to develop a new ecumenical understanding of the relationship between ecology and economy. Although the Canberra assembly did not mention the Kairos movement, it endorsed its aim by stating that the year 1992 should be emphasized as a year against racism with specific focus on indigenous and black peoples.

In taking this positive attitude towards the conciliar process the Canberra assembly corrected the negative judgments of many church leaders on the way grassroots groups and movements had involved themselves in the conciliar process. In theological terms one can say that Canberra acknowledged that the Holy Spirit does not only act through church dignitaries, but is actively present among the whole people of God.

The State of the Ark: Lessons from Seoul

Douglas John Hall

Even months after the world convocation on "Justice, Peace and the Integrity of Creation" ended, churches and others interested in the course of Christianity in the world were still endeavouring to assess what really transpired during this week-long ecumenical gathering in the burgeoning capital of South Korea. In Europe particularly, press coverage of the event was rather negative. As one who not only participated in the convocation and in numerous consultations leading up to it, but also strongly *believed in* the "JPIC Process", as it was called, I wish to add my support to those who are determined to think *positively* about the convocation.

I believe that the only responsible way of assessing the world convocation is to address openly the *problems* that surfaced in that assembly. For most of them reflect the state of the Christian movement today; they are not peculiar to Seoul. Part of the lasting importance of the convocation is that, being arguably the most significant *ecumenical* gathering in the modern epoch, it was the occasion for gaining a new awareness of certain difficulties inherent in ecumenical Christianity today — difficulties that are less conspicuous, naturally, in regional and other ecumenical gatherings that do not achieve the comprehensiveness of Seoul; difficulties that for the most part have been insufficiently acknowledged and addressed. There are *lessons* to be learned from Seoul. But the lessons will only be learned if we are honest about the problems that came to the fore there.

In this brief article, I intend to identify and comment upon five such problems. They are:

1. Global theology and contextual commitments: Is it possible for churches which have (rightly!) begun to engage in theologies that are consciously contextual to work simultaneously towards a pertinent global confession of Christian faith today?

2. Democracy and expertise: Having made some admirable strides towards a representative and inclusive approach to theological and ethical decision-making, how shall the churches employ those in their midst who through vocation and training possess expertise in a variety of fields?

3. Transnational faith and the preservation of cultures: Is an international, *world*-conscious faith like Christianity still concerned for the preservation of particular cultures and nations?

4. Interfaith dialogue: In view of the willingness of most Christians to acknowledge and respect other religious traditions, how shall we overcome the hesitancy of the churches to encourage full participation of those who are "not of this fold"?

5. Thought and life: Having discovered the limitations and dangers of disengaged theory and doctrine, can we reclaim serious theological thought for the life of the churches?

1. Global theology and contextual commitments

Perhaps the greatest frustration at Seoul was the failure to combine the quest for a globally appropriate profession of faith with commitments to theological and ethical positions that had been hammered out on the anvils of specific socio-historical contexts. Failure is not too strong a word in this connection. Given the aims of the JPIC process as it was conceived from the outset, the discussions at Seoul belie a stark problem for ecumenical Christianity which may require a great deal of time, understanding and compassion if it is to be overcome.

Clearly, the vision that inspired the JPIC process was an *ecumenical* one, namely the quest for a global Christian response to the realities of an endangered planet. From Vancouver onwards, the three prongs of the theme, "Justice, Peace and the Integrity of Creation"[1] were understood as dimensions of an indivisible whole. They were seen to imply a threefold threat to life, whose parts interact and constantly feed one another: injustice, war and violence, and the disintegration of natural processes. The primary message at Glion, the first *major* discussion of the theme after the sixth WCC assembly, concerned this uncanny interaction of the three "great instabilities" (Charles Birch). Repeatedly we heard (e.g. from Carl Friedrich von Weizsäcker): "There can be no peace without justice, no justice without peace, no peace or justice without vastly altered attitudes towards nature."

This sense of the interconnectedness of the three aspects of the JPIC theme is expressed faithfully in the "Second Draft Document", the document around which the Seoul meetings revolved. A brief extract from a long section of part I of the document, entitled "Interconnecting Dimensions of Our Present Crisis", secures the point:

> Our world is one cloth. As nations and peoples we relate to each other through our common response to the interlocking issues of justice, peace, and respect for the environment. To tear the thread of any one of these affects all of them together and shreds the whole cloth. Economic exploitation and political repression kill millions of people and will claim even more victims if they are not checked. The nuclear menace is a sword of Damocles suspended above humankind, and the continuing destruction of nature raises a question mark over the very survival of the species. But what is more significant in all of this — and what is grasped by too few people! — is that none of these threats can be combatted effectively if they are isolated from one another. The real danger lies in the fact that they are inseparably linked, and that it requires both knowledge and wisdom imaginatively to discern this linkage. In a society that rewards specializations and discourages holistic learning, such wisdom is rare! From now on, it must be consciously pursued and nurtured.[2]
>
> ...[to] most of us who come from countries which are ravaged by senseless wars, characterized by gross violations of human rights and by massive poverty and unemployment, the introduction of the item of the integrity of creation on our agenda seemed like a conspiracy by those who benefit out of our poverty and oppression, to divert and diversify our struggle for justice in our situations. It seemed like some people wanted to keep us busy with seemingly abstract concerns about the misuse of biotechnology rather than the real issues of land dispossession and racism, sexism, economic exploitation (classism), political oppression, and denial of the right to religious freedom and the use of religion as an instrument of oppression.[3]

Obviously enough, there are very divergent interests at work in this juxtaposition of approaches to the ecumenical task, and they must be forthrightly addressed. But a certain atmosphere of ecumenical etiquette (for want of a better phrase) prevails, rendering direct attention to such divergence almost impossible. In particular it is very difficult for "rich" Christians of the first (and to a lesser extent the second) world to engage in open disagreement with their third-world colleagues. Behind the scenes at Seoul, one could hear all kinds of implicit and explicit criticism of third-world "exclusivism" with regard to justice. "Do they not know that holes in the ozone layer jeopardize also their future?" one person asked. Privately and in small groups, it was felt by many half way through the week that the convocation might not survive the attempt (as it was perceived) to turn the whole discussion away from the theme as announced and towards justice *per se*. But this was not openly addressed.

If we are open to the lessons Seoul can teach us, then I think the very *first* requirement for ecumenical Christian dialogue today is that all participants must learn to distinguish between genuine solidarity with the oppressed, on the one hand, and the sort of passive public agreement that is born, not of Christian love, but of a combination of diplomacy, guilt and fear of conflict. And this lesson must be learned in particular by *first*-world Christians. The so-called third world, along with certain minorities in the affluent North, has found out how to say what it thinks — and to do so with relative grace and civility. Christians from Africa, Asia, the Caribbean and elsewhere no longer show up in ecumenical gatherings feeling that they must tell Europeans, North Americans and other "rich" Christians only what we like to hear. But we (and I refer in particular to the male of the species!) manifest such a fear of confirming all that is said about our fabled "machismo" that we are fast becoming incapable of *knowing* what we think, let alone articulating it in public.

But this freedom is accompanied by new forms of potential bondage. There is no non-dangerous theology! What if, while enthusiastically discovering the pertinence of the Evangel for the problems and pos-sibilities of our immediate situation, we were to lose touch with the larger historical tradition as well as with other provinces of the oikoumene? And what if, in our necessary preoccupation with the problems of our own "here and now", we were to lose sight of the *global* problematique in which our own problems are wrapped as in a blanket? Personally, I am deeply committed to contextuality in Christian theology and Christian life;[4] but that is the best possible reason for cultivating an informed awareness of the dangers of contextuality. To say it in a sentence, the real danger of contextualism is that it will devolve into the kind of regionalism or localism that threatens both the unity of the church and the unity of truth. With the reduction or demise of earnest attempts at global theology, we might see the emergence of a theological tower of Babel where, in contrast to Pentecost, the various provinces of "Christendom" could no longer communicate with one another.

Precisely *because* we have begun to think contextually, we are all the more in need of an ecumenical dialogue that can be a forum for testimony and interchange among many differing contexts. The old ecumenism asked how the separated *churches* might rediscover unity in Christ. The ecumenism that is called for now is one that asks how distinctive *worldly contexts*, evoking the need for distinctive articulations of the Christian message, may yet contribute to a Christian witness that is expansive enough to have global implications. To achieve such a new ecumenism, however, we shall have to learn not only how to be forthright about *our own* contexts and their quite explicit demands upon the faith; we shall have also to learn how to listen intelligently to the testimonies of those who speak out of socio-historical contexts very different from our own.

This leads to my *third* lesson, which seems to me to be directed to the churches both of the South and the North, though in different ways. It concerns our absolute need of one another. No one — certainly no one person, but also no one ecclesiastical province or grouping — can even understand the problems we face, let alone derive "the answer". Such comprehension can only be attempted communally and ecumenically.

Here, the testimony of the oppressed is vital. For not only do they point to truth about the world that the world seeks desperately to avoid — truth accessible only to the victims; but they also prevent the whole witness of the koinonia from becoming merely rhetorical and theoretical. It was *necessary* for third-world Christians at Seoul (and I mean necessary for *truth*, and all who would testify to it) to insist upon bearing witness to the unspeakable injustice that stalks the earth today. It was not the vocation of those who represent oppressed peoples to speak about the degradation of creation that is brought about by technological and other "leaderless" (Martin Buber) processes at work chiefly in first-world societies. *Of course* third-world people know about the depletion of the ozone layer! But that is neither what they should nor could emphasize in such an assembly. In the disciple community, moreover, it belongs to the spirit of grace and truth that those who suffer most immediately and acutely should be heard *first*.

There is however also a kind of testimony to truth that requires greater distance from immediate pain. When the (relative) material abundance of Northern peoples can be divorced from greed and aggressiveness; when their (relative) freedom from poverty and oppression is seasoned by compassion, they sometimes manifest a capacity for wisdom and fore-sight — that is, for the kind of thought about the world which depends upon a sufficient distance from personal and immediate suffering to consider hidden obstacles to the life that God intends.

May we not suppose that "in Christ" such wisdom is possible? I do not ask of all oppressed peoples, but I do ask of all *Christians* that they consider the possibility that "the integrity of creation" was introduced into ecumenical thought at this juncture in history, not by people who intended, purposely or by default, to detract from the concern for justice, but by people who used the gift of a little distance from pain in order to alert the church and the world to threats to planetary existence which, though less conspicuous perhaps than war and poverty, are not less threatening to *all* creatures. This was the first time that a major ecumenical gathering of Christians addressed itself to the grave questions of the environment; and it was all the more necessary to do so because Christianity itself has been partly responsible for the crisis of the biosphere. To have staged a world convocation of Christians on the subjects of justice and peace alone, and at this time in history, would have been irresponsible in the extreme. *Whoever* sets out today to address the great negations by which the future of the earth is jeopardized must address all three of these problems, both in their distinctiveness and in their inseparability. Is it necessary to choose between emphasizing one or other of them or attempting to see them whole? Is it not possible that a religious community that for twenty centuries has lived with the mystery of the unity-in-triunity of its deity might have acquired some insight for maintaining distinctions whilst honouring indivisibility?

2. Democracy and expertise

Throughout the approximately five years of active preparation for Seoul and at the convocation itself, the churches called upon persons who were qualified in a variety of disciplines to contribute to a deeper understanding of the theme. Approximately sixty such "experts", representative of a variety of disciplines including the natural and social sciences, economics, medicine, religion and theology, were present at the world convocation itself in the capacity of "advisers". We sat in a block of seats at the side of the large gymnasium in which the plenary sessions were held. Although, presumably, all of us contributed to the discussions in small "working groups", conspicuously few spoke on the floor during sessions of the plenum. For the most part we were silent. Looking about the group during plenary discussion — and especially during the almost two-day period when ten "affirmations" had to be voted on, sentence by sentence, by all delegates — one frequently noted expressions of frustration and sometimes sheer capitulation. Gradually, as they became a little acquainted with one another, the "advisers" exchanged verbal and non-verbal messages in which their incredulity, dissatisfaction and confusion over what was happening "on the floor" were prominent themes.

Why were the "advisers" not used at Seoul?

There is no easy answer to this question. To begin with, it must *not* be laid at the doorstep of the organizers. That kind of explanation is not only unfair to the hardworking and dedicated JPIC staff and planning group; it almost deliberately skirts the real problem.

I am not wise enough to offer a profound answer to this profound question, but I think that any really weighty response to it would have to entail a complicated study of the "democratization" of the churches from about 1960 onwards. At least within the so-called "liberal", "mainline" Protestant churches, we have moved in a very short period of time from a situation in which office and expertise were still prominent (consider the preparations for Evanston!) to one in which every decision must be arrived at, every sentence crafted by *everybody*.

This is why *preliminary* work — including the many consultations that preceded Seoul, some of which were excellent — hardly informs the great assemblies in relation to which it is "preliminary". Not only that, but it is even frequently regarded with suspicion! Apropos the latter remark, it has been widely noted in reports about Seoul that there was a great deal of criticism of the "Second Draft Document" — a document which collected findings from dozens of preliminary meetings and tried to present them in some semblance of meaningful language. Again and again it was said during the convocation that various groups had not had "input" into the document (although it would be hard to conceive of a document more inclusive in both its genesis and its content!). What one has to realize, I think, is that, given an atmosphere of what has come to be known as "participatory democracy", *any* document would have been criticized at Seoul. Because the real problem consisted in handing people a ready-made statement about the theme — and this is confirmed by the fact that the *part* of the document that was most sharply criticized (part I) was the part that the assembly was not invited to change, but only to comment upon. Most of the serious critics of the document really wanted Seoul to *produce* a document, one in which everybody (all six or seven hundred) had a hand, and in seven days!

Those of us who can remember when decisions were made by the relative few who held office in the churches or had achieved recognition as theological experts (overwhelmingly men, of course) are not likely to lament the passing of certain well-known aspects of that past. So beholden were "ordinary Christians" to the (largely unannounced) hierarchy of expertise and authority that few ever dared seriously to contradict the findings of these "leaders". Generations of women, young people, students, laity and parish clergy have sat quietly and listened whilst the experts told them about the state of the world and the meaning of the faith. It is perhaps poetic justice that this scenario is now vastly altered, some would say reversed.

But decision-making by everybody also has its problems. Not everybody is a scientist capable of understanding atomic energy; and not everybody is an ecologist, with all the background that is needed to grasp and explain "the greenhouse effect"; and not everybody is an economist, able to juggle all the factors that contribute to the national debts of nations like Brazil.

Nor is everybody a biblical scholar, ethicist, church historian or theologian. In the bad old days, some of us used to write books in which we insisted that every Christian is by definition a theologian and encouraged people in the church to lay hold to the claim. Sometimes one suspects that this lesson was learned too easily, by some. Certainly every Christian who is a Christian intentionally and not just through convention feels driven to "understand" what he or she "believes" (Anselm). Certainly every Christian who attempts to *live* the faith must also *think* the faith. And certainly every Christian who participates in the "body of Christ" has both the right and the duty to enter into the process of decision-making that determines the course of the "ark" called the church. This is a Protestant principle that was too dearly won to let drop! But to take up the vocation of a biblical scholar or a theologian or a church historian is to enter upon a life-time of disciplined and intensive study and struggle — a struggle just as demanding in its way as that of the professional musician or the brain surgeon. After nearly two thousand years of tradition, to aim at anything like expertise in the profession of systematic theology, for example, is to commit one's whole energy to a work of understanding that (as one knows from the outset) will never be achieved.

Recognizing the need for specific vocations within the Christian community by no means implies a return to government by expertise (insofar as such a thing ever really existed). For the most part, history regularly demonstrates that experts are very inept at government. It also shows that they, being sinners like all the rest, are tempted to use the power of their expertise for selfish ends. Democracy is in part always a safeguard against the will-to-power of those who are reputed to *know*!

But is there no way of combining the participatory approach to Christian community with an intelligent use of those within the body who have pursued special callings and may possess, therefore, special gifts? If we cannot find some way of doing this, then I submit that the churches are bound to become increasingly confused, shallow and contradictory — particularly when they take on, as they must, being witnesses to incarnate Love, great worldly problems such as those implied in the theme of "Justice, Peace and the Integrity of Creation". Without a great deal of *worldly* expertise, it is not even possible for us to ask the right questions where the "great instabilities" behind the three prongs of this theme are concerned. And without biblical, theological and historical expertise, the churches will cut themselves off from the wisdom that has been accumulating over two millennia — wisdom that we need, not only for intellectual acumen in the face of these threats to life, but for spiritual courage even to allow them into our consciousness.

The silence of the "advisers" at Seoul should be recognized as a danger signal in relation to tendencies present throughout the churches today, particularly throughout Protestantism. We may have overcome the immaturity that trusts expertise too much. But we have not achieved the maturity that is ready to acknowledge the need for expertise.

3. International faith and national identity

A very curious thing happened at Seoul. I do not know how widely it was noticed or how it was interpreted generally; but in my view it constitutes an indicator of yet another unacknowledged and unresolved question that is present within ecumenical Christianity today.

One evening was devoted to "Korean culture". After all, we had not gone to Seoul arbitrarily! During that evening, Korean dancers, drummers and musicians and other artists staged what I felt was a moving presentation of their national experience and aspirations. As a people capriciously divided on account of the struggles of great empires, they proclaimed through their art the yearning of the Korean people for reunification and self-determination. In a final pageant, one after another of the empires by which Korea's destiny has been controlled were expelled and the two Koreas embraced each other in an ecstasy of freedom.

Afterwards, when I expressed my enthusiasm for this performance I was met by a wall of dismay and resistance. Every European with whom I spoke about it had found the evening questionable. Some found it positively frightening!

Why? Because sensitive Europeans generally, and sensitive *Germans* in particular, can perceive nationalism only — or largely — in negative terms. Christian Europeans today think of their Christian faith as bolstering the movement towards a united Europe. By the same token, differently applied, many East and West German Christians manifest serious qualms now about the more militant and noisy side of the rush towards *German* reunification; for they remember the past of their powerful "Vaterland".

But what for one people may be a dangerous or presumptuous (if hidden) bid for empire may for another people, under different circumstances, be the only way in which they can summon the courage that is needed to *resist* imperialism. It was one thing for the Nazis to engage in much banner-waving and drum-beating at Nuremberg; it is something else for young artists in South Korea to beat their drums and exorcise the demons of their oppressors in energetic dance. The first is an exercise in *hubris*; the second is an exercise in *courage*.

Not all that is wrong with the world today stems from the desire of ethnic groupings to retain their sense of identity and dignity. The opposite danger may be more deadly in the long run. I refer to the coming-to-be of what the Canadian political philosopher George P. Grant called "the universal homogeneous state" — a better, because more comprehensive term than either "the technological society" or "the consumer society". Christians, who celebrate the varieties of creaturehood and the unpredictable adventures of historical existence, are unlikely candidates for the grey sameness that is being courted by subtle but powerful forces at work in the world today.

It is true that the discipleship of Christ calls us to embrace the universal, and in a way that is today inclusive not only of all *human* beings who are "other" but of whole species and ecosystems. But translating this discipleship into a specific sort of internationalism (often with ideological overtones!) is not the only way of obedience to the One in whom there is neither bond nor free, male nor female, etc. I am a Canadian nationalist *because* I am a Christian. I think that the best way that I can serve the large human and extra-human community, the globe, is by attempting to act responsibly within my own society; and acting responsibly within *Canadian* society today — a society that is being torn apart by apathy, ethnic and linguistic chauvinism, and the great magnetic pull that issues from the American imperium — means seeking to preserve what is best in Canadian history, culture and experience, and to resist (like my Korean brothers and sisters) the co-option of my rich and (yes!) "different" society by what the world (too lightly) calls "Americanization".

The challenge that Seoul issues to the churches through the medium of this cultural event is to manifest a form of *ecumenism* that is not just a stained-glass version of the *cosmopolitanism*[5] of the "universal homogeneous state"; an ecumenism that treasures the variety of gifts that are brought, not only by individuals, but by nations and peoples for the enrichment of the reign of God.

4. Interfaith dialogue?

At several of the preliminary conferences (especially, in my experience, at Granvollen in Norway, one of the best consultations in the process) representatives of other religious traditions were both present and vocal. At Seoul they were present.

Whether any of these others were officially invited to speak I do not know. I do know that during the plenary sessions they did so, on their own initiative, only rarely. I cannot imagine — from the general tone of what I heard from the *Christian* participants — that the visitors belonging to other faiths felt overwhelmingly bidden to enter the fray. At the final service of worship, which was in other respects very moving, it would have been a splendid and meaningful symbol to have had one of the Jewish representatives read the lesson from the older Testament in Hebrew. This did not occur. At the end of that same service, I noticed a Jewish representative sitting alone in obvious — and I suspect very *lonely* — thought.

We have come to a stage in ecumenical Christianity which it seems to me is quite dangerous in regard to all this. Because we have learned (somewhat!) that we do not have to be afraid of these others; because we have come to know enough about their faiths to realize that in many things they are not only not our enemies and competitors but may become close friends; because we have discovered that they are glad to be with us and almost always graciously accept our invitations; we seem to think that we have achieved interfaith dialogue! If we have achieved anything, it is limited to sheer physical proximity to some of the other religious traditions — on an occasional basis. We have by no means achieved dialogue, or even the beginnings of understanding who "they" are.

5. Thought and life

One of the standard epithets by which a great deal of intellectual labour is now regularly dismissed within the churches is the charge that it is "abstract". To this it is popular in certain circles to append the adjective "masculine". True to form, this was precisely the assessment put forward, almost from the outset, at Seoul, and applied, of course, to the previously mentioned and much-maligned "Second Draft Document". The document was alleged to be "abstract, masculine *[männliches]* thinking". It was asserted openly on the floor by one speaker that it must certainly be the work of "a European male".

It was not. It was the work of a great many men and women, only some of whom were European. As the *second* draft (and "second" is in this case really a euphemism for fourth or fifth!), it incorporated all the major complaints and suggestions that had come to Geneva from the widespread preliminary mailing of the *first* draft. Over two hundred written responses from every part of the world, some of them sizeable documents in themselves, were taken with great seriousness in this revision. The document was, of course, presented with some attempt at ordering ideas and securing transitions between contributions that had come from widely diverse sources; for it had to become the basis of a discussion among six or seven hundred people. But the judgment "abstract" could only, I think, be made by persons who have little acquaintance with closely reasoned (and in that sense abstract) theological writing — for example Schleiermacher's *The Christian Faith*, or Rosemary Ruether's *Faith and Fratricide*, or Dorothee Sölle's *Christ Our Representative*... or perhaps the gospel of St John.

It is obvious that here, again, we have to do with the problem (discussed earlier) that arises whenever prepared documents are presented to bodies with a high sense of "participatory democracy". But what is at stake here is also more than that. There is a certain *resentment* of thought abroad in the churches, and ecumenical Christianity must face this honestly and seek to correct it.

This resentment is not without its justification. Too much of the past thinking of Christian intellectuals has been theoretical and "academic" in the extreme. Still today amongst "the stricter sects of German theologians" (a phrase coined by Reinhold Niebuhr) there is a tendency to assume that any alleged theology that can actually be read by non-professionals is unworthy of serious attention. Some theologians still vie with one another for obscurity. Even in North America, that centre of pragmatism, where some of us have tried consciously to write theology that is accessible to *the churches*, the guilds to which we belong are suspicious that we are mere "popularizers". Profundity of thought, it is assumed, is incompatible with simplicity of expression (an assumption which makes one wonder how either Jesus or Socrates ever managed to do it!).

Moreover, such *theoretical* thought is never just innocently "academic" and irrelevant to life. It is frequently dangerous! Not only does it regularly translate into ideology, to which the world and the church must then be made to conform, but it often camouflages reality by substituting alleged universals for existing particulars. Generations of Latin American Christians were prevented from noticing their highly particularized forms of economic oppression and cultural colonialization because they were taught to imbibe eternal theologies whose universal truths were manufactured in Italy or Germany or Spain or France and should have been so marked!

Thus for a variety of very valid reasons the resentment of thought is understandable, and those of us within the churches who think for a living should not be surprised if we cast shadows not our own. All the same, to dismiss verbal or written theological reflection as "abstract" is not, in the long run, the wisest way to combat the evils of intellectualism. When so much serious and faithful and scholarly work is greeted with such an *a priori* bias, a situation is *courted* which may be seven times worse than the household cleansed of the demon of "abstraction". For when acts and ideas and impulses are no longer subject to the rigours of scholarship, it is almost inevitable that arbitrariness and wilfulness will take over, led by the most powerful and the most wilful. A church that resents thought stands a very good chance of becoming a thought-*less* church.

The truth of the matter is, of course, that thought is by definition abstract, if by abstract one means standing back a little way from the thing to think about it, reflect on it, see its implications for all manner of other things, and decide how best to proceed. One has to abstract from experience in order to understand, or even mentally to absorb, the experience; and one does this, invariably, whether one expresses one's thinking in complex discursive prose, as did Kant and Hannah Arendt, or in poetry, as did Elizabeth Barrett-Browning and Annette von Drost-Hülshoff, or in sophisticated novels like those of Doris Lessing or Margaret Atwood, or in "simple" parables like those of Jesus of Nazareth.

The test of authenticity where thought is concerned is not whether it entails this mental "stepping back from" life, but whether the end result of such an act of transcendence is a contribution to the living of life — to life's "abundance". Some thought, it is true, functions mainly to isolate people from life, or to give them the heady sensation of control. Is that why we are hearing the combination of the adjectives "abstract" and "masculine"? It *is* the case, I think, that a characteristic of man in Western civilization has been to seek, through ratiocination, to escape from and, simultaneously, to achieve mastery over life, with all of its terror and unpredictability. Because men have been expected by the stereotypes and patterns of our civilization to take charge of life, they have also learned how to escape from the mandate, for it is an awesome and finally an impossible one. Men are not gods! Thought can be and has, therefore, frequently been a neat and (yes) masculine sort of sorcery combining in remarkable ways the seemingly antithetical but curiously compounded impulses to escape and to master.

But thought is much greater than *all* the uses to which it has been put in a world that is alienated from its Source. And if as Christians we believe ourselves to have been put into touch again, in a beginning kind of way, with that Source; and if we are even ready to call that Source, amongst other things, Thought, Reason, Mind, Word (Logos), then may we not also suppose that *our* thought, when it is obedient, may serve, enhance, enrich and preserve life — that it may become "flesh"?

* * *

Truly, many problems emerged at Seoul. But they are not and should not be regarded as Seoul's problems! They belong to the Christian movement at this stage in its historical pilgrimage. They describe in some real way the state of the ark.

NOTES

[1] It seems to me very unfortunate that both the German and the French forms of the JPIC motto fail to capture the splendid nuance of the English (and Spanish) concept, "integrity of creation". The German *Bewahrung* and the French *sauvegarde* both connote something that *human beings* do in relation to creation; *integrity* on the contrary suggests that there is a certain "wholeness" inherent in the order of creation as such, and that human beings are called to respect and foster this.

[2] *Justice, Peace and the Integrity of Creation: Between the Flood and the Rainbow*; "Second Draft Document", part I,IV,i, para. 59. While the attempt to think "holistically" both about the world problematique and Christian response to it informed the central thrust of the process, it was difficult all the way through — and particularly at Seoul — to prevent the breakdown of this attempt through the singling out of one aspect of the theme. In particular, third-world delegates insisted upon the absolute centrality of justice, and their inclination to regard the other two prongs of the central theme as matters of concern to the powerful and the affluent came very close, often, to suspicion that peace and the integrity of creation (especially the latter) were first-world interests, whose primary function was to camouflage the realities of global injustice.

[3] World convocation document No. S.2, p.7 of typescript in English. Secondly, all Christians will have to recognize the limitations and dangers of theologies which are contextually engaged, and the way in which these limitations and dangers necessitate the emergence of a new kind of ecumenism. The contextualization of theological thought which has occurred in all "provinces" of the church universal is perhaps the most significant and exciting aspect of the Christian movement today. After centuries of theologies that were supposed to be eternal and universally applicable but were, most of them, made in Europe, we have witnessed the beginnings of a marvellous freedom: the freedom to think the faith in conscious dialogue with the specifics of one's own place and time; the freedom to engage the realities of this world as they are experienced concretely *hic et nunc*, and to do so from the perspective of a gospel that is not simply imported from the past or from the struggles of other peoples but emerges out of the lively dialogue between "text and context".

[4] See in particular my *Thinking the Faith: Christian Theology in a North American Context* (Minneapolis, Augsburg, 1989). As churches, we do not possess as such the expertise that is necessary for a detailed and profound comprehension of the complex world in which we live and the enormous, interlocking factors by which its future is threatened. But we do have — or may receive! — something more important than expertise; and that is the prospect of sufficient *trust*, *modesty*, and *openness* that we may dare to "reason together". There is perhaps no other collectivity in the world today that can draw upon the resources of mutuality, ultimate concern for the earth, and historical hope that are there for those who expect the reign of God. It was in fact this sense of Christian universality (catholicity), combined with the belief (as Seoul put it) that "the world belongs to God" and is "beloved of God", that lay behind the vision that was articulated in the words of the Vancouver assembly of the WCC, "Justice, Peace and the Integrity of Creation". In the midst of this world's Babel there is a "pentecostal" movement which from time to time is able to make good the grace that transcends the language of self and considers, in love, the whole.

[5] I owe this distinction to Toshitake Noma, professor of economics in Doshisha University, Kyoto, Japan. Yet on every one of the three prongs of the theme, and on the aforementioned difficult subject of their indivisibility, *all* the representatives of the other faith traditions at Seoul might have contributed much to our Christian comprehension. Think of the Buddhist and Hindu traditions of respect for "the integrity of creation"! Think of the Jewish and Islamic history of contemplation on the nature of justice! Think of the wisdom of indigenous peoples in North America, Australia, New Zealand and elsewhere in maintaining peaceful boundaries of respect between human and extra-human forms of life! The wonder of the Seoul theme, given our all-too-myopic Christian past, is that it was by definition inclusive: it is not explicitly and narrowly "Christian", despite its obvious pertinence to the living of the Christian life today, and therefore it opens itself naturally and without artifice to all others of good will. But while we asked them to come to Seoul, we did not seek wisdom from them. By its neglect, Seoul places this lesson also on the agenda of ecumenical Christianity.

A *Latin American Perspective* on the JPIC Process

Brenda Consuelo Ruiz Perez

To introduce my presentation, I would like to share a personal experience with you. I teach Sunday school to the six, seven and eight year-old children in my local church in Nicaragua. Our literature comes from the Baptist Publishing House in El Paso, Texas. A few Sundays ago I was supposed to teach the children about how God loves them and provides them with food and clothes, and the toys they play with.

I decided not to teach that lesson because I knew some of those children don't have enough food to eat, clothes to wear or toys to play with. I wasn't sure I could explain to them how an unjust national and international economic order affects their lives in spite of God's love for them.

Our situation

I would now like to invite you to take a short trip with me, starting with the part of the world in which these children live. This is a country like many others in the third world, where one finds poverty, injustice, struggle for survival and, in spite of them, faith and hope.

Take a look at what I am wearing right now.

• This is the text of a presentation made at the WCC's seventh assembly in Canberra in 1991.

1. This is a Nicaraguan native dress and it is made of cotton. Cotton is one of Nicaragua's major exports. As in other Central American nations, thousands of acres of land have been taken away from small farmers who produce basic foods. This land is used to produce cotton that will help pay our external debt.

To make the fields more profitable, millions of gallons of pesticides (banned in the United States and other developed countries) are spread over the cotton-growing areas, leading to devastating environmental damage. Central American babies, through their mother's milk, consume between six and 207 times the acceptable amount of DDT according to the World Health Organization.

The previous owners of the land, now reduced to labourers, are paid extremely low wages and live and work in sub-human conditions. Many of them go to the urban areas seeking a better life but end up living in slums. For lack of adequate skills, many take to prostitution and crime to make a living.

2. This is a necklace made out of coffee beans, another of Central America's most important sources of income. The by-products from the processing of coffee and sugar cane, as well as from chemical industries, have heavily polluted most of our water resources. Jesus' expression "rivers of living water" used in John 7:38 and 39, is a metaphor that can hardly be used in Central or most of Latin America any more, since most of our water supplies bring death, although slowly, to our population. The international prices paid for our products have become lower and lower, making growers and other business people less willing to invest in ecologically safe processing methods.

3. I am also wearing a wooden bracelet made of lumber, out of one of Nicaragua's endangered precious species of wood. The Atlantic coast was a region known for its wealth in lumber, mineral deposits and seafood as well. It is here where the majority of our remaining indigenous groups live. Since 1894, thousands of acres of trees have been cleared from the region by North American and European lumber companies, with no concern for reafforestation. Some of the environmental consequences of this have been a massive erosion of the land and drastic changes in the eco-system, which have caused both flooding and drought in different parts of the country.

Lumber was not the only thing the companies took from the land. They also took countless tons of gold, silver and tin, leaving behind a handful of wealthy businessmen, rivers poisoned with mercury, and thousands of workers sick with tuberculosis and living in extreme poverty. These people, with one of the highest levels of unemployment in the country, have survived through the over-exploitation of the land, hunting and fishing, bringing about the extinction of dozens of animal species. There is also a very high incidence of alcoholism and drug abuse in the area. Fernando Cardenal, a Jesuit priest and the ex-minister of education, once said: "When one does not have anything to eat, one eats the future."

It is important to point out here that many of our Latin American governments come to power and stay in power because they work for the interests of the transnationals and to make money for themselves, at great cost to the people. A discontented population, created by this situation, is held under control by these governments only through severe military repression.

Such was the situation in Nicaragua until 1979 when, after a long and bloody struggle, the people took over power and made an attempt to build a society in which the interests of the transnationals would no longer come first, but rather the needs of the poor. Massive literacy and vaccination campaigns were launched; hundreds of schools, health-care and day-care centres were built, and widespread land reform started to take place.

This was considered, primarily by the United States government, a "bad example" for other third-world countries. In an effort to erase the Nicaraguan revolution, the US government started what they euphemistically called "low intensity warfare". The civilians were the first to suffer the consequences of the US economic embargo. The hardest hit by the budget cuts in health care, education and social welfare made to fund defence expenditure, were women, children and other poor.

The eight years of the Contra war, which was condemned by the International Court of Justice in 1986, caused incredible human suffering to the Nicaraguan people, leaving thousands dead, disabled, orphaned and war-displaced. The direct and indirect environmental damage is staggering. The economic losses have been estimated to be the equivalent of 45 times Nicaragua's yearly income from exports. However, the US government has yet to abide by the world court's ruling and pay for the damage done to the Nicaraguan people.

4. Here I have a bracelet made out of a cow's horn and on my feet I am wearing cowhide sandals. Another of Central America's main exports to the first world is meat. This also helps pay our external debt. To produce that meat, our countries have had to engage in massive destruction of our tropical forests, a very important part of the world's breathing

lungs, to turn them into grassing fields, what is now known as the "hamburgerization of the forests" which is a major contributing element to the "greenhouse effect" from which the whole world will be suffering within a few years.

But we are the ones who are already suffering the short-term effects of these measures. Now that the land has been used for cattle grazing, the soil has been impoverished to such a degree that it can no longer be used for producing foodstuffs, which has led to the further impoverishment of the population.

It is rather ironic that in Latin America, where we have the natural resources necessary to satisfy the basic needs of the population, one finds such a high concentration of the world's poverty and hunger. According to the Kissinger Commission's report in 1984, about half of the urban population and up to three-quarters of the rural population in El Salvador, Guatemala, Honduras and Nicaragua, could not meet their basic needs in terms of food, housing, health and education.

5. I am also wearing coloured beads around my neck. These beads are similar to the ones the Spanish invaders gave our indigenous peoples in exchange for our gold, silver and precious stones five hundred years ago.

As many prepare for the anniversary of Columbus' arrival on our continent, we in Latin America must continue to deal with the effects of the plundering, genocide and ecocide that took place during Spanish domination. It has been calculated that with all the wealth that has been taken out from our countries by the first world since the time of the conquest, plus all the interest we have paid, our external debts would have been paid three or four times over.

That is the situation in Latin America, and in many ways it is very similar to that in other third-world countries.

Final considerations

I would like to end this trip by asking you to take a look at yourselves right now.

The cotton your clothes are made of may have come from Nicaragua, Guatemala or India.

Your watch may be made with metals that perhaps came from Chile, Bolivia or Zaire.

The coffee, bananas, cocoa and sugar that are part of your breakfast may have come from El Salvador, Colombia, Brazil or Kenya.

The medicines that some of you take may have ingredients that were taken out of our tropical forests.

The paper you use and the furniture you have in your home may have been made from wood that came from the rapidly disappearing forests in Costa Rica, Nigeria or Thailand.

If each time you eat a hamburger, drink some coffee or look at your watch, you think of all the living things (human and non-human) that have suffered in the process of producing those things, then you will realize how unjust our world is.

Land, wealth and power are unequally distributed, and the distance between the two extremes grows every day. Rich countries become richer and poor countries become poorer. The third world is poor because the first world is rich, and they are rich because we are poor. But our survival depends on them and their survival depends on us.

We can hardly understand such a world without recognizing how conflict arises and how, in turn, it gives rise to repression and death. We need to listen to the voice of the blood of millions of brothers and sisters, children and adults, as well as to woods and rivers, crying from the ground; and we need to ask ourselves: "Am I my brother's and sister's keeper?"

As a church we need to recognize that we have failed to do what God has called us to do. We have failed to be stewards of God's creation. Not only have we not defended the oppressed and exploited, but we have often taken sides with the oppressors and exploiters. We have been very eager to preach about peace without giving thought to justice, as if we could have one without the other and as if creation could be restored without them both.

As we come together and meditate on the WCC's Canberra assembly theme: "Come, Holy Spirit — Renew the Whole Creation", we need to remember that it is through us that the Holy Spirit will renew the creation. Yet, only when we start thinking in terms of one world instead of a first, second and third world can the whole of creation be renewed. We all breathe the same air, we all drink from the same water source, and we are all nourished by the same soil. Therefore, together, as one world, we need to take care of this creation, God's creation.

If you take a last look at what I am wearing today you will notice my dress is green. In Latin America it is the colour of hope, and it is our hope and faith that my Sunday school children and all the children and peoples will see the glorious creation as envisioned by Isaiah:

> ...no more shall the sound of weeping be heard in it, or the cry of distress. No more shall there be in it an infant that lives but a few days, or an old person who does not live out a lifetime;...

They shall not build and another inhabit; they shall not plant and another
eat;...
They shall not labour in vain, or bear children for calamity; for they shall
be offspring blessed by the Lord... (Isa. 65:19-23, NRSV).

So I invite you now, with much hope, faith and love, and in the name
of those who have died in their struggle to build a better world, to engage
in a conciliar process of mutual covenant in the seeking of justice, peace
and the integrity of creation.

From Basel to Seoul and Back...

JPIC as a Process of Ecumenical Learning for European Churches

Rüdiger Noll

It seems to be the fate of ecumenical, especially socio-ethical, programmes and initiatives that they come and go, but seldom stay very long. At the beginning of an initiative there is enthusiasm because the ecumenical movement (very often only sectors of it) seems to have found an adequate response to a certain challenge. In a second phase of "realism", obstacles, tensions and confrontations emerge increasingly. And finally, since the obstacles cannot be removed immediately, the programme gets stuck. This certainly limits the programme's impact on the life of the churches as well as on society at large (crisis of the ecumenical movement). Yesterday it was JPSS,[1] today it is JPIC and tomorrow...?

When the joint working group on JPIC of the Conference of European Churches (CEC) and the Roman Catholic Council of European Bishops' Conferences (CCEE) met in June 1990, members observed a decreasing interest in JPIC on a European level. Have we already reached the stage at which JPIC is going to disappear from the list of priorities of ecumenical bodies, churches and networks? I find this rather astonishing. At a time when governments increasingly recognize their responsibility in the UNCED[2] process, which one could regard as a secular JPIC process, on the churches' side there is a decreasing interest in commitment to similar, ecumenically defined goals and their implementation. The search for mutual commitment seems to be the main stumbling block for many churches to embarking on an effective process of reception of the Basel European assembly and the Seoul world convocation.

To avoid misunderstandings: once established, ecumenical programmes need evaluation, and new developments might require redefined priorities. This article should be understood as a contribution to such an evaluation from a European perspective, at a moment when the World Council of Churches has just undergone a restructuring process and is developing future programme priorities, and when the Conference of European Churches is preparing for its tenth assembly, its highest decision-making body. For most of the churches, which are involved in the process of redefining programme priorities of ecumenical bodies like CEC and WCC, it is a matter of choice, not of chance, whether and in what form the conciliar process continues.

The European churches have done their homework...

The Vancouver call to JPIC received much attention in Europe. In 1983 Europeans felt especially threatened by the fact that the Cold War was reaching a new climax and more and more resources were being spent on arms production. War seemed to have again become a political option. It was with this background that the German philosopher and scientist Carl Friedrich von Weizsäcker mobilized people in (then) West Germany and beyond, when he called for a council for peace and for a word from the churches which the world could not fail to hear.[3]

It was first of all the groups and movements from within the churches[4] which committed themselves to the JPIC process as it was formulated in Vancouver: a process of mutual commitment (covenant) for Justice, Peace and the Integrity of Creation — not emphasizing peace issues only. In most of the Central European countries it was these groups and movements which challenged the churches and their decision-making bodies to join in. Consequently, local and national initiatives got started. In some countries, especially the German-speaking part of Europe, real processes were set in motion which led to documents defining how to approach national priorities within the JPIC framework. In the case of the former German Democratic Republic, for instance, this process had quite a remarkable impact on the "non-violent revolution".

The different local and national approaches found their focal point on the European level in the European Ecumenical Assembly (EEA), "Peace with Justice", which was held in Basel, Switzerland, in May 1989. For the first time since the schism of the eleventh century, all major denominations including the Roman Catholics came together in a huge assembly.

The Conference of European Churches and the Roman Catholic Council of European Bishops' Conferences were co-inviters. In a process of mutual ecumenical learning it was possible to break the barriers of confessions for a common witness, facing today's challenges.

During the preparations, the character and the size of the EEA developed. An effort was made to take into account as vast a scope as possible of different experiences in various contexts. No less than six hundred responses were received to a first draft document from churches, organizations, groups and individuals. When the EEA started, church delegates brought another five hundred suggested changes to a revised second draft.

The EEA was originally planned as a meeting of two hundred participants, but it grew significantly to include many thousands of people. Seven hundred representatives were delegated by their churches and bishops' conferences, among them 38.7 percent women and 9.7 percent youth. In addition, there were fraternal delegates and guests from other continents. European networks established a programme of hearings; groups and movements set up a "market on the future of Europe" and visitors from all over Europe and beyond joined in. At Pentecost 1989 Basel was a place of sharing for the "whole people of God" — a process which most of them had never experienced before.

During the assembly the participants reflected on the challenges before them, witnessed to their common faith, confessed their sins, developed a vision of Europe, formulated basic affirmations and entered into concrete commitments. The final document, "Peace with Justice for the Whole Creation", is the synthesis of this process. It was adopted by 95.4 percent of the delegates. It is based on an unprecedented process of consultation and participation and can be called "the most comprehensive and inclusive statement of the European Christian peace ethic".[5]

Although it was a European process, right from the beginning the approach to the issues was a global one. The chapter on the vision of Europe in the final document is framed by the following sentences: "For many people elsewhere this relatively small part of the world called 'Europe' does not stand for the quest for human dignity, freedom and social justice, but for colonial expansion, slavery, racism, discrimination, economic exploitation, cultural domination and ecological irresponsibility."[6] "As churches in Europe as a whole we must advocate that this opening of the borders within Western Europe not lead to a 'Bastion Western Europe', closing itself more and more towards the rest of the world."[7] Similarly, the participants endorsed a recommendation of the

Brundtland report that the industrialized countries should reduce their energy consumption by fifty percent in order to allow the third world to increase its energy use by thirty percent.[8]

One can say that, motivated by this unique process, the European churches did their homework.

... but did not pass the final test

The Basel assembly represented also a stimulation for all kinds of activities of European Christians and churches in relation to JPIC. The Protestant churches of Austria serve as an outstanding example as far as the highest decision-making bodies of a church are concerned. Their synod decided that the Basel final document should be their future guide for decision-making and action. The Swiss churches ecumenically announced a jubilee year during which they quite successfully fought for a debt release for the world's poorest countries by Swiss authorities. Steps were taken to reduce the greenhouse effect and to search for alternatives to the military service of young men.

The seriousness with which the churches dealt with major issues of today made them interesting conversation partners for scientists and politicians. Political parties asked the churches to enter into dialogue with them on the practical consequences of the Basel decisions. The document was handed to Mikhail Gorbachev by Patriarch Alexy of the Russian Orthodox Church when Gorbachev had just started his reforms. In 1991 the president of the Swiss Confederation, Flavio Cotti, said: "I endorse the Basel appeal and commend it to the whole nation."[9]

Before and after Basel, it was mainly the churches and groups in German-speaking countries which embarked on the process. Three years later, one can observe that new initiatives are emerging in other regions while the process has lost its momentum in the former centres of activity. In Sweden, for instance, secular as well as church-related groups came together for the first time this summer in the framework of JPIC in order to establish links and action plans.

Groups and movements have nevertheless continued their commitment to the process and established networks on a pan-European level. Kairos-Europe — which counts more than six hundred member groups today — is taking action on issues related to the year 1992: the five hundredth anniversary of the colonization of Latin America by Europeans, and the year in which the Single European Act is supposed to be established. At Pentecost in May 1992, representatives of marginalized and solidarity groups assembled for a People's Parliament in Strasburg,

France. The European network for JPIC — to cite another example — brings together those organizations which took part in the hearing programme at the Basel assembly. It publishes annually material for a Week of Prayer and Action for JPIC and tries to share information by issuing an occasional information bulletin.

That these groups and movements felt the need to establish their own platform witnesses to the fact that in most cases it was not the churches as a whole which committed themselves to continue the process. Only certain sectors of the churches tried to implement what was commonly adopted at Basel. The churches as a whole were rather selective and took up what would fit into their own agenda, setting aside whatever could have challenged their own approach and their own structures. For the committed segments of the churches this was a disappointing development. Only recently a leading member of Kairos-Europe put it very clearly: "Kairos-Europe was formed in Basel in 1989, because it was foreseen that the majority of the European churches and communities would not accept the binding character of the conciliar process. Meanwhile it has become clear that, at best, they accept the concept of the three dimensions, i.e. recognizing, judging and deciding/acting, but they go no further than the rhetoric and are not ready to draw the consequences for their own structures and social action."[10]

A gap developed between the basic willingness of the churches as a whole *to act* and the stage of implementation. Thus, the churches did do their homework, but they did not pass the final test.

Lessons from Seoul

When the world convocation took place in March 1990 — less than a year after the European Ecumenical Assembly — it was not clear how the conciliar process would continue in Europe. Most Europeans, representatives of churches as well as of movements, came to Seoul stimulated by the spirit of the Basel assembly, well prepared and with a clear agenda but, perhaps, wrong expectations. Those who expected that Seoul would lead to the "word of the churches which no one can fail to hear" got the impression that Seoul was a failure.[11] They were disappointed that Seoul did not reach the same kind of coherence in the analysis, the theological reflection and commitment as did Basel. But how could it? Seoul took place at a time when participants from other world regions did not have the same opportunities to prepare themselves. There was discrepancy on the global level as far as entry-points to the process and methodologies were concerned. The situation in a restricted region such as Europe is more compact.

Nevertheless, Seoul was indeed a decisive step in the process and Europeans could learn many lessons from it.

Seoul prioritized the issues of justice, peace and the integrity of creation in a different way from the Europeans. It assembled firm convictions of faith and revealed some questions of principle which need to be clarified in the ecumenical movement.

The most important outcome of Seoul was that it demonstrated *how* justice, peace and integrity of creation are inter-related. "If JPIC wants to touch the root causes of most of the issues, justice issues have to be at the centre of the conciliar process," said a People's Forum preceding the world convocation. "Injustice", according to their definition, "is the unjust accumulation of wealth and power." The message of the People's Forum belongs to the important, but forgotten, texts of the JPIC process. Its contents can be found here and there in the final document of Seoul, but the proposed document on the common analysis which could be read as a response to the People's Forum was not adopted in Seoul, for other reasons. One very clear message from Seoul is that European churches have to tackle issues of economic justice. Especially in the year 1992 with the attempt to concentrate economic power in Western Europe, these statements remain a major challenge on the churches' agenda.

Beside the issue of economic justice, the "affirmations" of the Seoul document touch on other crucial issues. However, they do not really contain anything new. The affirmations confirm basic human rights extended to basic rights of God's creation as a whole. But in the way they summarize a long ecumenical discussion and present its results as "firm convictions"[12] of churches, they represent a unique document. Some people called it a "catechism of ecumenical social ethics".[13]

Contrary to a widespread opinion, catechisms are not primarily meant to serve as a guide to distinguish between orthodoxy and heresy. Seoul never intended to exclude people who do not subscribe to the affirmations. Catechisms, in the historical sense, are a means of stating firm convictions in order to stimulate an adequate human response and encourage their implementation in the life of the churches. This way, the affirmations of Seoul represent the result of a process of ecumenical learning and at the same time a stimulation for the continuation of this process, with *action* as its goal. One definition of ecumenical learning says: "Ecumenical learning is a process by which:
— diverse groups and individuals
— well rooted in their own faith, traditions, cultures, contexts
— are enabled to risk honest encounters with one another and before God

— as they struggle and study together in community
— with personal relevant issues
— in the light of the scriptures, traditions of their faith, worship and global realities
— resulting in communal action in faithfulness to God's intention for the unity of the church and humankind, and for justice, peace and the integrity of creation".[14]

Following this definition, it seems that Seoul achieved a preliminary summary of the results of the common struggle and study on relevant issues. But the JPIC process still lacks the "communal action" as it is mentioned in the definition. Or, to say it in the terminology of liberation theology, the community gathered at Seoul succeeded in presenting, in its affirmations, a clear analysis and a judgment in the light of the gospel, but the action is still missing. Seoul was therefore not the end of the conciliar process. The affirmations represent most valuable guidelines for the ongoing process.

Four priorities were chosen by the global ecumenical family in Seoul which require immediate action, if humankind does not want to miss the kairos: the oikoumene must struggle for a just economic order, a comprehensive security system, protection of the earth's atmosphere and racial justice.

Facing these priorities, it is evident that a process of ecumenical learning on these issues cannot be a never-ending process. "Conciliarity" in this context means aiming at decisions and actions as quickly as possible. "Now is the time...!" was the key phrase of the message from Seoul — more than two years ago! In the plenary, in which these priorities were adopted, it was recommended that the seventh assembly of the World Council of Churches in Canberra should review the actions which had been taken. However, this follow-up of Seoul never took place. Maybe Canberra was too early for that, but when will this evaluation be done and who will take the initiative?

The European JPIC process after Seoul

Although there were a number of challenges for European churches, it was not long after Seoul that the CEC/CCEE joint working group on JPIC observed a decreasing interest in JPIC. This, of course, does not mean that there is a decreasing interest in JPIC-related issues, but in JPIC as a process which tries to link the issues and tries to develop a mutually committed ecumenical fellowship of churches and networks around the world. The reasons for this are many.

First of all, Europe underwent drastic changes which actually started a few months after Basel, and in Seoul nobody yet had a clear idea of what the future would look like in Eastern Europe. It turned out that what was often celebrated as the liberation from communism and centrally planned economy, for many people in Eastern Europe, became a struggle for daily survival. There was no energy left to get involved in global ecumenical programmes. Most remarkable under these circumstances, the churches in the former GDR explicitly saw their involvement in the peaceful revolution as their contribution to the conciliar process.

An adequate response from Western churches is still missing. It seems that only Eastern Europe "needed" a revolution while the West can continue without any change and celebrate its "victory". The developments in the East occupy the agenda of the West, without questioning that the model of free-market economy failed to prevent people from starving and to sustain God's creation. The groups and movements in the West which are committed to the struggle for economic justice and sustainable development felt unheard and unsupported, as if the document adopted in the conciliar process never demanded action on these issues. The dichotomy between words and action is only too evident. Grassroots people who embarked on the conciliar process with some hopes are caught in a feeling of powerlessness. But although those who are committed to the conciliar process often feel excluded from the decision-making process in church and society, there is no resignation. Many examples witness to the fact that the process is going on and many initiatives are encouraging people to join in.

JPIC as a process — the next steps in Europe

The debate about the term "conciliar process" did for a long time emphasize the word *conciliar*. This was and still is important, since the concept of conciliarity and covenanting made the difference between JPIC and former socio-ethical efforts of the ecumenical movement. Today, however, after the big assemblies of Basel and Seoul, it is more important than ever to recall that JPIC from its very beginning was defined as a *process*. Nobody could expect that Basel and Seoul would solve all the problems. They were *decisive steps* on the road to an ecumenical community committed to justice, peace and the integrity of creation, but they were *not goals* in themselves. Signs of the time rather indicate that we are further away than ever from justice, peace and the integrity of creation. Latest statistics show an even greater number of starving people in the world than in 1983 when JPIC was created.

UNCED revealed the unwillingness of the Northern states to take appropriate action for sustainable development. Violence and war are the results of national and ethnic conflicts in Europe, although the Basel final document says: "There are no situations in our countries or on our continent in which violence is required or justified."[15]

The ozone layer is being depleted and although there is a growing consciousness among people, which led to changes on the consumer side, political parties and industries have done very little to reduce the greenhouse effect. With these facts in mind, it sounds rather cynical and/or can be seen as a sign of resignation in view of the extent of the problems, if efforts and resources for the JPIC process are diminished. If the implementation of once-adopted commitments is regarded as being less important than the formulation of documents, JPIC will have the same fate as other ecumenical programmes and gradually disappear from the churches' agenda. What is needed *more than ever* is perseverance and a joint effort of all sectors of the churches to renew their commitment to the JPIC process.

The CEC and the CCEE on the European level have already announced publicly their willingness to keep the process alive. As the organization of the Basel assembly was a joint effort, the reception process is also being undertaken ecumenically, including all major denominations represented in Europe. In addition, following a decision of the advisory committee of the CEC, the follow-up work on the Basel assembly should be carried out in co-operation with representatives of other religions rather than only interdenominationally.

The CEC and the CCEE established a working group on JPIC with the mandate to monitor JPIC initiatives in Europe, to enter into deeper reflection on crucial issues and to encourage further commitment. The working group recommended that "CEC and CCEE commit themselves actively to work towards the convocation of a second European ecumenical assembly in 1995 or soon after. This will provide new energy and give an impulse to further ecumenical activities at various levels." In the meantime both the CEC and the CCEE announced that they will convene an EEA II certainly before the end of the century.

On the way to an EEA II, the working group is trying to establish study and action programmes on what one could call "generative themes", i.e. issues which touch existential problems and offer entry-points for people to participate. Three of these study and action programmes are under way. The first is called "Towards a Culture of Non-violence" which for the time being emphasizes the problems occurring in the conversion of arms industries. The second, "Global Crisis and JPIC Process", tries to evaluate and promote the basic values carried in the JPIC process. Finally, the third project on "The Churches' Responsibility for Environment and Development" tries to provide an input from the European churches to the UNCED reception process and to spell out the churches' responsibility in the North-South conflict within Europe and on a global level.

However, all these projects cannot be carried out by two ecumenical bodies with rather limited resources. The success of any process depends on the co-operation of those who are already involved or want to get involved in the JPIC process and the work on a local or national level. The ecumenical institution can only offer support, co-ordination and communication facilities, and perhaps some stimulation.

NOTES

[1] JPSS stands for the ecumenical programme for a "Just, Participatory and Sustainable Society", which was launched at the fifth WCC assembly in Nairobi, 1975, and not followed up after the WCC central committee meeting in Kingston, Jamaica, 1979.

[2] UNCED is the abbreviation for the United Nations Conference For Environment and Development, Rio de Janeiro, 3-14 June 1992. But instead of speaking of a conference, in relation to UNCED, one should rather see it as a process. Preparations for the Earth Summit took more than two years and a reception process has just started. As part of the follow-up, for instance, there is the intention to develop an Earth Charter to be presented to and adopted at the United Nations' fiftieth anniversary in 1995. UNCED can be regarded as a secular JPIC process since it concentrates — like JPIC — on the following areas of concern: development (economic justice) and care for the environment.

[3] Cf. Carl Friedrich von Weizsäcker's speech at the "Kirchentag von Düsseldorf", West Germany, in 1985 and his book *Die Zeit drängt*, Carl Hanser Verlag, München-Wien, 1986, p.11.

[4] With this formulation I want to indicate that I regard groups and movements as being an integral part of the church. If I distinguish in the following between groups and movements on the one hand and the church (in the sense of church leadership and structures) on the other, it is to clarify their different commitments to JPIC.

[5] Roger Williamson, "The Basel Document: Its Development and Adoption", in *Peace with Justice*, the official documentation of the European Ecumenical Assembly, Basel/Switzerland, 15-21 May 1989, published by the Conference of European Churches, Geneva, 1989, p.66; and Volkmar Deile, "From Stirling to Basel: The Preparation and Organization of the European Ecumenical Assembly", *ibid*.

[6] Basel Final Document, §46.

[7] Basel Final Document, §62.

[8] Basel Final Document, §87d.

[9] Interview with President Flavio Cotti, Katalog 91, published by the Swiss Bishops' Conference, Bern, 1991, p.4 (unofficial translation).

[10] Ulrich Duchrow, "Kairos Europa", *Ökumenischer Informationsdienst*, no.2/1992, p.2 (unofficial translation).

[11] Cf. the press release of the German Protestant Press Agency, 13 March 1990, with the headline "Das Friedenskonzil der Kirchen ist gescheitert" (The peace council of the churches has failed).

[12] Introduction to the ten affirmations in the Seoul final document.

[13] Cf. e.g. Volkmar Deile's introduction to the final document of the world convocation, WCC, Geneva, 1990.

[14] *Alive Together: A Practical Guide to Ecumenical Learning*, Sub-unit on Education, WCC, Geneva, 1989, p.8.

[15] Basel final document, §61.

Women in the JPIC Process

Women in many parts of the world were deeply involved in the JPIC process. They were committed to the goals of JPIC, and their contribution to the world convocation was rich and varied. They prepared themselves for the convocation through a series of regional meetings which served as a forum to articulate their concerns and gave an opportunity to grow in awareness and solidarity.

We publish below extracts from a report of these regional meetings.

* * *

BREAKING THE SILENCE

Priscilla Padolina

Sub-unit's response to the Vancouver call

Vancouver gave a call "to engage the churches in a process of mutual commitment to justice, peace and the integrity of creation". Recognizing women's deep concern and commitment in the struggle for JPIC, and that they have a real contribution to make, the Sub-unit on Women has designated JPIC as a programme focus. Under this area of concern, three points are emphasized.

1. Justice for women: reflecting on the issues of violence against women, especially on the feminization of poverty, women under racism, women refugees, and migrant women workers.
2. Women for peace: affirming the new innovative voices and actions of women as peace-makers and peace-keepers, and the new models for engagement in political change.
3. Women committed to caring for God's creation.

At its commission meeting held in Mexico in 1985, the Sub-unit was mandated to organize a series of regional meetings in Africa, Asia, the Caribbean, Latin America, the Middle East, the Pacific, Europe and North America. Six of these regional meetings have since taken place. Reports on these meetings have been produced and widely disseminated.

The objectives and the participants

In each of the regions, the following objectives were suggested, but it was left to the regions to adapt the objectives according to the situation:

1) to analyze the socio-political and economic implications of the lack of justice and peace and the destruction of nature in the world;
2) to analyze the interlinkage between sexism and militarism/militarization; to expose the effects of militarism on women;
3) to document the innovative contributions of women to justice and peace-making efforts and their efforts in the area of ecology;
4) to build solidarity networks between women of North, South, East and West;
5) to discover what the Bible says to women as initiators of justice, peace and the integrity of creation.

Women in the struggle for justice, women engaged in peace movements, women committed to caring for creation, and women doing theology were brought together to share their stories of pain and struggles, their hopes and aspirations to build a better world. Together they explored feasible actions for implementation at national/regional level as they discovered their power and strength. It has also paved the way to build a common bonding of sisterhood and solidarity around the world. The journey to Seoul which spanned five years (1986 to 1990) involved 610 women in these regional meetings.

Signs of hope?

The coming together of women through sharing their experiences in the struggle helped them to discover that they share a common oppression. This new consciousness of their common suffering gives them the inspiration to dream dreams and share visions. African women who participated in the first JPIC meeting held in Gweru, Zimbabwe, in 1986, on the theme "Working Towards a Just Society" articulated their vision thus:

Our Vision of a Just and Peaceful Society

One in which there is nurture and support for growth of our potential, that is — mind, body and spirit — where there is equal access to resources; and where every person can participate fully in the process of decision-making on all matters which affect our lives, individually and collectively.

One in which there is a system of just distribution of resources, without exploiting some sections of society.

One in which there is awareness of the importance of nature and the environment and a sense of responsibility to protect it from destruction and exploitation.

One in which basic education is available to all, and continuing education is accessible to all who wish to have it.

One in which power is shared through the delegation of responsibility and sharing of knowledge and information.

One in which the structures and constitutions accommodate the needs of the people and adapt to changes in the society.

One which is loving, caring, understanding, sharing — where the gospel is practised.

As women we envisage a society where we can be ourselves; where our gifts are valued and recognized; where we have the power to influence policy for choices towards peace, not war; where women's voices are heard and respected, whether in the church, village or government; where women take part in the decisions concerning the allocation of resources at all levels; in the church, in the community, in the nation.

In the Pacific (Tonga 1987) the theme of the consultation was "Caring for God's Creation". One of the biblical reflections was on the creation stories — that God created the world as a harmonious whole, that we human beings are partners, co-creators with God in the use and care of creation. The Pacific women composed the "Pacific Women's Creed" to express their confession of faith in their own context:

We believe that creation is a gift of God, an expression of our Creator's goodness.

We believe that as human beings we are part of this creation and that we share in a special way in the creative power of God.

We believe that the resources of our lands and waters and air are precious gifts from our Creator, to be used and looked after with loving care.

We believe that there is a rhythm to God's creation, like a drum beat; when we lose the beat, or the drum is damaged, the music is out of tune.

We believe that in order to be good stewards of creation, we have the responsibility to seek information on important concerns of our people and our region, and to share information in our communities.

We believe that like flowers we can bloom fully only when we are planted in God's love.

We believe that women have the right and the duty to give glory to the Creator by developing their full potential for the serving of their communities.

We believe that we are called to work not in isolation, but in community linked with women in their local situation, in our Pacific region and internationally.

We believe that we can rely on the strength and support of each other, to build on the common concerns we share, to go beyond the boundaries which separate and divide us; united we stand.

We believe that as Christians we are called to be peace-makers, in the true peace which God promises us.

We believe that this may sometimes mean "disturbing the peace" as Jesus did, for a purpose — to restore the purpose of God.

We believe that our Pacific ways are also a gift from God; we are invited to use the values of our Pacific culture to build societies of justice and peace.

We express these beliefs, reminded of the love of God, the grace of Christ, and the fellowship of the Holy Spirit.

Amen.

In San José, Costa Rica, a sub-regional meeting was held in 1987 in which women from Nicaragua, El Salvador, Honduras, Guatemala, Panama and Costa Rica participated. The women interpreted their vision of JPIC on a piece of cloth where they portrayed a region without boundaries.

One of the concrete actions for follow-up of the Asia JPIC meeting was a recommendation "to explore the feasibility of setting up a commission to monitor human rights violations of women in Asia, to mobilize world action in support of women in the movements". Their argument for the urgent need of such a commission:

In the traditional human rights discourse, there was no place for women because crimes against women were understood to be domestic issues; therefore, these crimes were denied their public face. In its exclusion, it left out the experiences, the wisdom and visions of women. Rape in prison, sexual dimension of torture, prostitution, feminization of poverty and so on cannot be classified as violence against women. There is therefore an urgent need to challenge the existing human rights concepts from a feminist perspective. To look with new eyes, through the eyes of women, through the eyes of those who have been on the margins.

Seoul — JPIC women's forum 1990

Seoul was a high point in the JPIC journey, but not the end. Prior to the world convocation, a JPIC women's forum was held. More than two hundred women from all corners of the globe came together at this event. The aims of the meeting were: to build community among the women, to familiarize them with the issues so that they could participate fully in the deliberations/decisions at the convocation. The theme of the forum was "Women Affirming and Women Covenanting". Two Bible studies were presented in a creative way which incorporated music, dance, visual aids, anointing with oil and affirming each other. Other creative interpretations of "Covenanting" were done in art, drama, song and poetry. We share with you a poem, "A Cry from the First World", which expresses an important message. It was written by Nansie Blackie.

And where has beauty fled?
And the frail bud of joy?
The primal gifts of Eden do not survive the death of innocence.

The incubus of history sprouts guilt around our necks like chains —
But Eve must not — like Adam — shift the blame:
Dear Lord, forgive that we compound the crime
With alibis like governments — or men —
Or even ancestors, whose ignorance had in itself a kind of innocence.

O Lord forgive us, as our guilt inhibits action.

Have we permission to rejoice in mountain, sky and flower?

May he whose heart warmed to the hills, the flowers — and sparrows —
Grant us the grace to *feel* forgiven.

The journey onward

The feminist movement, though it takes on different emphases in different contexts, is global. Its starting point — women's experience of suffering and struggle — has opened up a new consciousness. Women have begun to search for their roots from the underside of history, bringing to the open the present suffering, struggle and creativity of women as they look forward to a more holistic vision of life in the future. Feminist theology, which is also rooted in the experience of women, is part of the movement. It uses the telling of stories, drama, dance, music, poetry and art — which express this new feminist paradigm. In doing theology this way, we have discovered the richness of our gifts and the contribution of women towards creating a just and renewed world.

The Ecumenical Decade of the Churches in Solidarity with Women, which was launched in 1988 by the WCC, is a focal point to give visibility to women's perspectives and actions in the work and struggle for JPIC. We urge the churches to take actions in solidarity with women, so that the vision of a renewed community of women and men will become a reality.

Women have now broken their silence. All around the world women's networks for actions in solidarity with women have spread their "nets" from one community to another, across the islands and nations, in the regions, and around the world.

More than six hundred women have been engaged in the regional meetings. They will bloom where they are planted, but they will not bloom in isolation. They will link up with the millions of women who are engaged in the struggle for JPIC around the world.

People's Participation and the JPIC Process in Asia

Kim Yong Bock

People are subjects of history

Participation of a people has its roots in the life of the people themselves. People came before structures; social structures were created to serve the people in circumstances that developed out of their history. These structures were often misused to subjugate the people by those in power, and those in authority created arbitrary structures to further dominate the people. But people continued to assert themselves, to struggle for their life and to create their own future. The accounts of people's participation in history have become part of the traditions of people.

The struggles of the people have taken different forms: rebellion, resistance and revolution, according to their historical circumstances. Their perception, grasp of historical realities and their visions have varied accordingly. There is a rich reservoir of wisdom that has accumulated out of people's sufferings and struggles.

Such experiences and wisdom cannot be easily systematized; rather, they have to be shared through forms of communication such as stories. Theories on people's participation must be subject to their experiences and wisdom. Religious doctrines, political ideologies and social

---

• This paper was written before the break-up of the Soviet Union.

philosophies and sciences are to be discerned in terms of their usefulness to the people.

Within this framework we seek to discover people's participation in recent Asian history. People participated in their traditional rural political economy. They realized socio-economic security in their communities, with creativity in common living. When times were difficult, they faced crises and disasters together, through co-operation and sharing. When there was unbearable exploitation and oppression from above or outside, they resisted and rebelled against heavy taxes and imposed burdens. Often, however, they had to bear these burdens with patience.

When the colonial powers of the West and the East penetrated the communities and kingdoms in Asia, people had to defend themselves and their religio-cultural and national identities and socio-economic security. They involved themselves in struggles for national independence and self-determination. Sometimes they had to use the tools of the colonial powers to resist their domination, as the leaders of the independence movements were often trained in the West.

After the second world war, people hoped that the new "independent" nation-states would bring freedom, justice and prosperity. The nation states were led by the leaders who struggled for national independence and liberation. The perennial question was how to re-link their modernization programmes with the former colonial and Western powers. Some advocated socialist modernization, others capitalist models, and still others mixed economies with a liberal polity.

In this process of so-called modernization, numerous problems arose. Industrialization and urbanization led to rural impoverishment; there was rising alienation, and discrimination against ethnic and national minorities. Political oppression and violation of human rights were becoming more and more common, as was discrimination against women and the young. All these problems were intensified through the global Cold War conflict and the climate of confrontation between the two military super-powers which penetrated every aspect of the life of the people. Often the national security forces functioned against the security of the people.

The global situation from the perspective of Asian peoples

A. *Impact of perestroika on Asian nations:* The drastic and rapid change taking place in the world has several dimensions. The most immediate change is taking place in the Cold War order. The policy of perestroika in the Soviet Union is not only transforming the Soviet society and the societies of the Eastern bloc countries; it is also drastically altering the global order, from the Cold War rivalry to a new "security(?)" structure for the East and the West. In the short run these changes are being resisted in China, North Korea and a few other Asian socialist states.

B. Erosion of the Cold War order and its many dimensions: Such changes in the socialist states and in the global order challenge the Western policy of containment and confrontation with the Soviet Union and its socialist allies. The security policy and military establishment of the United States and its alliances with the Western nations such as NATO, US-Japan and ANZUS and other nations have rapidly become "redundant". This will have a considerable impact in terms of the security arrangements among Asian nations. For example, there will be a change in the security situation and the relationship between socialist and capitalist nations in Asia.

C. Common European house: Europe-centred world? Furthermore, the common European house is emerging as the dominant economic power, and will grow rapidly for the next ten years following the introduction of the market system and the 1992 economic integration of the European community. This will seriously affect the economically weaker sectors of the global village, particularly its southern half. Some Asian nations, such as the newly industrialized countries, may participate in the economic surge in Europe; but most of the Asian people are likely to suffer more economic hardship than ever before, for world resources will be drawn to Eastern and Western Europe.

D. Transnational corporations will penetrate Asia: The next decade will experience the so-called technetronic revolution on a global scale, as is already apparent in some Asian countries. This had been predicted already in 1970 by none other than Zbigniew Brzezinski in his *Between Two Ages*. The transnational corporations of the Western nations will now penetrate all societies, socialist or capitalist, developed or underdeveloped, with their technetronic logic. It will dominate the military, the bureaucracy, economic organization and communication media and control the total life of people from far-away places.

E. Exploitation of higher values by the powers: The dramatic disintegration of Cold War bi-polarization will further erode the doctrinaire ideologies, both socialism and capitalism. Already there is a greater trust in the pragmatic approach to economic and social policies. However, the pragmatic approach alone will not be adequate to deal with the deeper and more universal questions of humanity. Hence the need to focus on the question of universal values, not as ideological expressions, but as transcendent ultimate references.

In this context the political, economic and technetronic powers will seek to exploit the universal and transcendent values, both religious and secular, to legitimize their hegemonic powers. The values of Asian religions, as well as of the Christian faith will be mobilized by the powerful to justify established political powers, as political ideologies will be discredited as ultimate references.

People look for a new future — and democratic participation

It is not only the socialist states that aspire to make democratic reforms. In the nations of Asia such as Burma, the Philippines, Pakistan, Korea and Taiwan, people are expressing in a variety of ways their aspirations for democracy. In a similar way, African people are seeking to overthrow one-party dictatorships. Also Latin American people are seeking to establish the "civil society", by overthrowing the militarized one. All this is evident not only on the political level, but also on the levels of peace movements, consumers' movements, ecology movements, women's movements and minority people's movements. The people's movements for participation are the central thrust of Asian history today.

Asian people are learning how to live together as communities — even though there are frequent eruptions of communal and national conflicts. What the world needs is a trans-racial, trans-ethnic and trans-religious solidarity which is truly an ecumenical bond for justice, peace and the wholeness of heaven and earth. Justice, peace and the integrity of creation can be vitally related to the religious traditions of Asian people.

People's participation in national contexts in Asia

A. *The nation-state as the centre of power in Asia:* The life of the peoples in Asia as well as in other parts of the world has been determined by the power configuration in the nation-state. Some states are heavily dependent upon other political and economic powers within and outside the nation. Even though religious and cultural influences may come from outside, as well as from within, to effect changes in the nation-state, at present it is the current nucleus around which the life of the people is organized.

B. *The secular and religious state in Asia:* Two factors determine the nature of the state: the first is religious or secular; and the other is socialist or capitalist. The demarcations of these have never been clear-cut; but they serve to clarify the nature of the state.

None of the traditional nations in Asia was strictly secular, and most of them had religious underpinnings. This means that the Asian people had much political wisdom in their religious traditions. This has been eroded by the Western concept of the secular state, which involves the idea of non-dependence on religious values as well as religious institutions. The secular states in Asia, as well as the religious or semi-religious states, followed the ways of the Western secular nations, seeking to modernize or westernize themselves. Recently there has been some revival or resurgence of religions, which has implications for the nature of the state. Islam in Pakistan, Indonesia and Malaysia, Hinduism in India, Buddhism in Sri Lanka and Thailand, Christianity in the Philippines, Australia and New Zealand, and Shinto in Japan have become political influences to the extent that these religions affect the nature of the state and the political life of the people.

C. Westernization and modernization of the state: This trend is countered by the concept of the Western secular states, capitalist and socialist, which seeks to separate the state from religion. The socialist states have gone on to define religion as destructive to society. Now this is being challenged in the East European nations. This trend is likely to emerge in Asia as well. The countries that adopted capitalism on the economic level have been practising "pragmatic atheism", where the economy runs without religious influence, although some countries seek to apply religious principles to their capitalist economies.

D. Religious values as the reservoir of wisdom in the search for an alternative human community: Under these we must discuss two aspects.

1. Religion in itself and its institutionalization (religion and power): Here we need to speak about religions on two levels: the first is the established institutional one, which is closely related to the reality of power and the powerful; and the second is a transcendent dimension, which is not related to the powerful institutions, but is closely related to the alienated people in their powerlessness. Religion that transcends the religious institutions and powers is genuine, for it seeks to transform the existing power structures by realizing the aspirations of the oppressed people, as well as by refusing to justify the actions of the powers that be. The problem with the resurgence and revival of religions is that they seek to be "political" religions holding on to power, directly or indirectly.

2. Religion and the political life of the people: Secularization of politics in Asia has not been a sufficient condition for the democratic

development of the people. Religions in Asia should serve the realization of the full sovereignty of the people in their political life. Often religions served the nation-states in their absolutization of power, which violated the sovereign rights of the people, particularly their basic human rights.

E. The sovereignty of the people: Asian peoples have been expressing their ardent desire for democratic participation in political life. This is manifest in different ways in movements in every nation. Religion can be a decisive factor at this crucial historical juncture of Asian political development.

F. National economy versus people's economy: The nation-states have become the basic units of economic development, socialist or capitalist. The role of the nation-states in this respect has often been over-emphasized leading to the violation of the socio-economic rights of the people. Many of them carried out successive five-year plans for economic development. Whether under capitalist development or socialist development, Asian people have not been able to deal successfully with hunger, poverty and injustice.

G. Search for people's political economy: Now the people do not want to discuss endlessly the relative virtues of capitalism and socialism, as they did during the Cold War period. They need whatever system will secure their socio-economic security, one that is agreed upon with their own participation. People cannot leave economics to the state planners, capitalists and experts. They must take charge of their own economic and social well-being.

H. Asian religions and people's political economy: This means that the wisdom of Asian religions can help the people as they develop a political economy for humane socio-economic security in their own nations. National economies as the basic units of people's economic life have up to now been subjected to internal political control and dependency upon external economic powers such as transnational capital. The common ecumenical search for liberative religious wisdom in the Asian religions in order to realize socio-economic security is an important ecumenical agenda for us, just as it is critically important to realize the sovereignty of the people in their economic, social and political life.

I. Technetronic power: The so-called modernizers, capitalists and socialists blamed Asian traditional religions for the ills of Asia and they dismissed Asian wisdom of the people as obstacles to progress. Secular rationality was regarded as the saving logic for historical progress, and technology as incarnated rationality was allowed to penetrate the economic process, statecraft and security apparatus. The consequence has been the subjugation of the people by technocratic powers.

J. Trans-religious solidarity: Christian theology of religion and culture has been arrogant and did not recognize the riches of Asian religions. But today Asian churches and the ecumenical movement, together with Asian religions, are behind Asian people in their struggle to shape their own political, economic and cultural life and destiny. Churches and ecumenical movements must have courage more than ever to enter into deeper sharing and dialogue with Asian religions in the present struggle for a common and shared vision of society.

Asian ecumenical agenda: for churches to serve the cause of people's participation

Initially the Asian ecumenical agenda was framed from a Western perspective. But gradually it became clear that the historical process of the peoples in Asia should set the agenda for the churches and the ecumenical movement in Asia. This is indeed a dramatic change. Churches and ecumenical movements in Asia sought to analyze God's word in the Bible in the context of the suffering and struggling peoples of Asia, and to shape the life and witness, ministry and mission of the churches in the same context. Theological reflections have been taking place in the midst of the struggles of the people, gradually replacing the Western theological traditions.

A. The people of Asia is the context; people are subjects of history: Within this context Asian churches and ecumenical movements took up the burning issues of the political and economic life of the Asian peoples on the one hand and the deep religious faith and cultural heritage of Asian peoples on the other. We have set our thinking, life and action as churches and the ecumenical movement within this frame of reference. We are making some breakthroughs in this respect in the ongoing work of the Christian Conference of Asia (CCA). However, in the light of the new global and Asian realities, we need to give some thought to emerging priorities for an ecumenical agenda in Asia.

B. Issues

1. Political vision: The democratic movements of the people in almost every nation in Asia as well as in other parts of the world demand a clarification on the nature of the democratic society, beyond the liberal and people's democracies, and on the nature and mechanisms for the full participation of the people.

2. Political economy: The socio-economic security of people is denied by capitalist societies. The so-called NIEs (Newly Industrialized Economies) in Asia promote the penetration and domination of the global capital, rooted in the West and Japan. We need to understand the nature of the economic violence they inflict on people. The socialist economies in the so-called second world and in Asia no longer serve as an alternative economic model of development for the people in Asia and in the third world. The rapid introduction of the market process in the formerly socialist countries in Europe, the market integration of the European Economic Community and the emergence of the European common house will make the global economic order sharply bi-polarized into the rich North and the poor South. The search for viable economic alternatives that will realize the basic socio-economic security of the peoples in Asia is an urgent task today, when neither capitalism nor socialism promises such a prospect for the people, denying as they do people's right to participate.

3. Justice and peace: The unity and solidarity of the human community should be realized in justice and peace. Here we may have to call for the dismantling of all violent security apparatus in every nation; and peace should be called for on the social level as well as on the international military level. This may demand a total ecumenical mobilization of peace traditions, particularly from Asian cultural and religious heritages. Asian people's peace movements will have to address the question of violence on all levels: economic, social, military and political, cultural and ecological.

4. Religious and cultural identity and freedom should be guaranteed: The doctrines of national security and economism (a mammonism — a doctrine that economy is the most important factor and all else can be sacrificed) have taken the place of supreme values in our societies. The secular culture of rationality in science and technology has become the norm. The invasion by the "modern" Western culture uprooted and suppressed the people's cultural identity and freedom in Asia. Christian theology played a destructive role in this aspect, identified as it was with Western culture. There should be a radically open approach by the Christian churches to the religious and cultural life of the Asian peoples.

5. Protection of life and its fulfilment: gardening for life: Here too the basic scientific and technological rational approach of Western culture, Western industrial economy and military strategy has created the threat to life on a cosmic scale. The Asian religious and cultural heritage should be

brought to make a critical contribution towards the building of the "Garden of Life for All".

6. Democracy and participation of the people: (a) Crises of democracies: people's democracy and liberal democracy: The so-called people's democracy has failed, for democratic centralism and centralized planning of the economy did not allow the people to participate. Liberal democracies are not the answer, for they cannot prevent the monopoly and domination of global capital by transnational enterprises; and they cannot control the globally operating military apparatus of the powerful nations. (b) Facade of democracy in the third-world countries: Traditional authoritarianism, authoritarian bureaucracy, despotism, and military dictatorships pay lip service to democracy. It is in this context that a search for a participatory democracy has a new relevance and immediacy.

Consequences for the ecumenical movement

Christian theology has been a fellow-traveller in the cultural journey of the West. Some Asian theologies celebrated the process of secularization brought about by Western scientific reason. Now Christian theology must be humble and learn from the religious and cultural wisdom of the Asian peoples. What are the consequences as we as churches and the ecumenical movement participate in the agenda of the people's struggle?

1. Articulation of a Christian vision in the context of the people's struggle in dialogue with religious and secular visions of society in four areas: (a) the political vision of people's sovereignty: (b) the vision of a political economy which will ensure the socio-economic security of the people; (c) the vision of peace, internal (national) and international; (d) the vision of the "garden of life".

2. Communication as the sharing of the common vision, wisdom and experiences of the people among themselves; communication for solidarity; communication as cultural action against cultural violence and domination.

3. Common action in solidarity: inter-linking solidarity and unity among liberation networks as a comprehensive and inclusive ecumenism beyond ecclesial ecumenism. Inter-cultural and religious solidarity, inter-religious and inter-ethnic solidarity, inter-gender solidarity, inter-generational solidarity, trans-caste and trans-class solidarity are some of the new ecumenical horizons. For this emerging ecumenical solidarity truly ecumenical communication is critically important, and a solid infrastructure for such a communication action network must be evolved.

4. The communication of the deep convictions and beliefs of Christian faith, while learning and respecting the convictions of Asian faith, must begin. Traditional evangelism should be understood in the context of this mutuality. The sharing of the gospel among Asian peoples cannot be pursued in the old style of Christian aggression and conquest.

The means to renewal

1. Reading the Bible in the context of the suffering and struggling peoples of Asia.
2. Articulating what we confess and believe in the Asian context now.
3. Reshaping our church life, order (leadership and ecclesial democracy, and administration of resources) and spiritual disciplines.
4. Theological reflections and ethical articulations for the life and mission of the churches; in particular Christian social ethics should address the Asian context.

Conclusion

We need to envision an inclusive ecumenical (conciliar) process in Asia in the context of our solidarity with the suffering and struggling peoples in Asia at national, regional and global levels.

The Asian ecumenical process should move from the grassroots, to the national level, to the regional level and to the global level. The Asian perspective must be operative in the global ecumenical process. The Asian ecumenical process cannot be a limited intra-ecclesial conciliar process for unity, but must express its solidarity with the Asian people's movements, whether these be religious or secular. A process of people's participation is the proper ecumenical milieu for Asia and indeed for the ecumenical movement as a whole.

"What God Has Joined Together, Let No One Put Asunder"

Reflections on JPIC at the Canberra Assembly

Roger Williamson

1. What were JPIC's prospects prior to the Canberra assembly?

No definitive judgment can, as yet, be passed on the ecumenical process on "Justice, Peace and the Integrity of Creation". The process was launched in Vancouver 1983, made a slow start and gained momentum in the second half of the inter-assembly period. The world convocation in Seoul (March 1990) was held less than a year before the WCC Canberra assembly. In this article, drawing heavily on the documents from the assembly, I show how JPIC is reflected in the final documents and indicate some possible paths for the future.

The title for this evaluation is taken from the marriage service. It has been my impression that the ecumenical process on justice, peace and the integrity of creation has been a serious attempt to bring together:
— theology, spirituality and social action;
— justice, peace and ecological concerns;
— contextual and universal approaches to church life and theological reflection;
— Christianity, other faiths and wider secular movements in dialogue and joint action on these issues.

As with a marriage, the question of permanence must be raised, the issue of the long-term commitment to keeping together what was brought together in the early days of enthusiasm or first love. Will JPIC prove to be a long-term and stable commitment?

A cursory look at the assembly programme and structure, for example of the kind which delegates had to make in advance of the assembly when deciding in which section to work, presented those committed to JPIC with considerable difficulties. There were four sections to choose from:
— Section I: "Giver of Life — Sustain your Creation!"
— Section II: "Spirit of Truth — Set us Free!"
— Section III: "Spirit of Unity — Reconcile your People!"
— Section IV: "Holy Spirit — Transform and Sanctify Us!"
Where should one who was committed to JPIC as a holistic approach choose to work? At first sight, it looked rather like this. Section I would deal with theology of creation (the "IC" bit), section II would do justice and peace (the "JP" bit), sections III and IV would deal with the ecclesiological and spiritual dimensions (the "ecumenical process" bit). The danger was that JPIC would end up like a cold roast chicken at a picnic, with each guest pulling off a favourite piece — a wing here or a leg there. Tasty and appetizing, but not good for the holistic perspective — or the chicken!

The second reflection was that it was probably both wise and necessary that those who planned the assembly should divide the sections under headings which did not allow an automatic "slotting" of current programmes of the WCC into the assembly structure. Otherwise, those who have worked on those programmes could try to ensure that the same programmes re-emerged strengthened, or at least more or less intact, in whatever post-assembly structure the Council ended up with. To provide an opportunity to "cut, shuffle and redeal" (to use a card-playing metaphor) was necessary.

The third reflection which I and others expressed was that there was frustratingly little opportunity to see how *anything* could be decided or clearly accepted at the assembly in terms of structure and programme. One attempt at restructuring the WCC had already run into the sand in central committee. There was no guidance given to delegates as to how the WCC structures would look after the assembly. Particularly those who were new as delegates could not have a very clear idea of how the WCC either functioned as an organization prior to the assembly or would be likely to function afterwards — in spite of the detailed and often excellent assembly preparatory materials. How were those who were convinced that the JPIC process had a very real promise, which was only partly fulfilled as yet, to emphasize the importance of JPIC for the future? The situation was compounded by indications from those responsible for assembly planning that clear proposals of a *structural* character would be ruled out of order, or otherwise blocked or discouraged? All that was agreed was that it would be necessary for the WCC to *have* a structure after the assembly. The assembly was, in effect, disqualified from having any views as to what that might be. That approach had a positive and negative side. The positive side was that it spared us from inflicting on ourselves plenary sessions in which alternative plans for reorganization were discussed. That would almost certainly have been even more confused and fruitless than some of the plenary sessions which we suffered in Australia. On the other hand, there was no real opportunity for arguing out the point that JPIC was one key element around which the reorganization of the Council could take place and testing that conviction against other views.

Thus, there were very real fears that JPIC would be endorsed — but effectively dismembered — and that even if the assembly enthusiastically affirmed that JPIC should continue, this carried no necessary weight with respect to *how* that should be done, whether finance and staff would be made available as a priority, and so on. A fundamental ambiguity of JPIC had bedevilled progress — that when things were going well and when it was convenient, JPIC was presented as a main programmatic thrust of the entire Council, but when it was struggling, JPIC was a small staff unit which could not rely on the full weight of the organization and its wide range of resources being mobilized to get things done. Now at the assembly, this ambiguity meant that, depending on which staff member one talked to, one could get the answer "JPIC will come into all the sections" or "it depends which bit of JPIC you are interested in, different bits of JPIC will come up in different places". In addition, there were various rumours around, as always on occasions when future policy is being discussed in the WCC. One in particular was that the difficult funding situation of the Council and staff changes meant that a separate JPIC co-ordinating office was a complete non-starter as an option.

In summary, then, one had the impression that the true state of JPIC prior to and at the assembly was that JPIC would be everywhere but nowhere in particular, and that bits of it would crop up in particular sections. Given that rather unpropitious starting point, the results of the assembly for JPIC are most encouraging, since it emerges as one of the clearest and strongest programmatic emphases for the forthcoming period. Whether this promising basis is realized depends, of course, on the decisions to be taken by the executive and central committees, on how these are implemented by staff, the strength of support for JPIC from the top of the organization, and, inevitably, the Council's financial situation.

2. The basic documents

For the purposes of this evaluation, the main assembly documents to be considered are:

— Reference Committee report;
— Section I report, "Giver of Life — Sustain your Creation!";
— Section II report, "Spirit of Truth — Set us Free!";
— Section III report, "Spirit of Unity — Reconcile your People!";
— Section IV report, "Holy Spirit — Transform and Sanctify Us!";
— report of the Committee on Programme Policy.

The section reports focus on their respective themes. These were summarized and brought together in the paper by the *Report Committee*, which is not considered in this study since it merely covers the same material in summary form. The report of the *Reference Committee* deals with the moderator's and general secretary's reports and ecumenical relationships, e.g. with the Roman Catholic Church, member churches, ecumenical organizations, etc. The public issues and resolutions on specific political situations, many of which have JPIC implications, are not considered.

A key point for consideration is how the Seoul covenant from the JPIC world convocation of March 1990 (emphasizing the debt crisis, militarization, the atmosphere and racism) and the ten affirmations were taken up in Canberra.

2.1: REFERENCE COMMITTEE

The clearest reference to JPIC in the *Reference Committee* report deals with a passage in the moderator's report, as follows:

> The Committee acknowledges the efforts that have been made to implement the request of the Vancouver assembly to develop a "vital and coherent theology" in order to bring into a coherent perspective the theological work being done in all the programmes of the WCC. Despite all efforts made so far, this task remains unfinished. The Committee suggests that the future development of a "vital and coherent theology" within the WCC should be in relation to the continuing JPIC process, BEM [Baptism, Eucharist and Ministry] reception and other basic tasks.[1]

2.2: JPIC IN THE SECTION REPORTS

It should be stressed that this is not a full evaluation of the section reports, nor even a detailed summary of their contents. This review merely indicates where JPIC was referred to specifically in those documents and relates this to the context of the discussion.

2.2.1: Section I, "Giver of Life — Sustain your Creation!"

The entire section report must be understood as a contribution to the ongoing work of JPIC — particularly the integrity of creation dimension of that work. One of the major debates with relevance to JPIC in section I was the extent to which anthropocentrism should be questioned in the report. Whereas the first draft of the report was greeted in the assembly newspaper with the headline "Central Place of Humans Questioned",[2] the final version toned down the approach considerably.

A clear recommendation was made on continuing work on the formulation of an adequate creation theology[3] — a task parallelled by the need for an ecumenical contribution to the United Nations Conference on Environment and Development in 1992 in Brazil.[4] Sustainability was taken as a key term in the reassessment of economics and ecology.[5] The third part of the report dealt with "Covenanting for the Life of All Creation"[6] and stressed that "the understanding of creation theology and of an ethic of economy and ecology should be reflected in the life and work of the church...".[7] It is thus logical when the report states that the WCC should:

> Continue the Justice, Peace and the Integrity of Creation process as a framework for study and action on these issues.[8]
>
> The churches should "act together in defence of life",[9] campaign for "protection of human life and for the preservation of the environment" and "for the abolition of the institution of war".[10]

2.2.2: Section II, "Spirit of Truth — Set us Free!"

As with section I, the report of section II is, in its entirety, a plea for the insights of JPIC to be incorporated into the life of the churches and for the process to be continued by the WCC. Specific references include the plea that "spirituality in unity should be held together with issues of justice, peace and integrity of creation in the programmes of the WCC".[11]

As a result, the WCC and its member churches were encouraged to "engage in dialogue with those in power at all levels — whether local or international — on the issues of justice, peace and the integrity of creation (JPIC)" and "support Christians engaged in working on JPIC..."[12] The verdict from the JPIC process thus far "confirmed the assessment that prevailing models of economic growth and world trade" do not create "conditions for a sustainable society".[13]

In the issue group working on racial justice, the relevant findings from Seoul were explicitly affirmed.[14] A similar approach was followed with respect to detailed recommendations (e.g. arms transfers, conscientious objection, denuclearization of navies) in the group working on "lasting peace and meaningful security". [15]

The recommendations to the churches stressed "regional solidarity", "ecumenical ministries for JPIC and shalom services", as well as "lay training, leadership formation and ecumenical learning" for JPIC. [16]

Recommendations for the WCC asserted that "the JPIC emphasis must be strengthened as a focus of WCC work" and that "the WCC should support regional 'peace networks' and monitor their co-ordination through an 'exchange centre' in Geneva". [17]

The group working on justice for women set their institutional focus on the Ecumenical Decade of the Churches in Solidarity with Women. In the plenary discussion, one of the points raised with great vigour was that the condemnation of sexual harassment should have been made more clear, particularly in the light of incidents at the assembly. The point was stressed by WCC president Lois Wilson (United Church of Canada), Rev. Mary-Gene Boteler (Presbyterian Church, USA) and agreed by co-moderator of the section, Margot Kässmann, who stated: "I wish we had strengthened the part of our report dealing with sexual harassment." [18]

The document closes with five common themes: human rights; the role of the United Nations; dialogue, gospel and culture; community; and power. [19]

Thus, the verdict of section II was that the entire JPIC process, in particular the Seoul covenant, was affirmed as giving direction to the WCC's work:

> The churches should commit themselves to the affirmations of the Seoul convocation. Justice, peace and the integrity of creation should continue to provide the orienting framework for church commitment to peace and justice. The Seoul covenant, with its stress on protection of the environment, alleviation of debts, demilitarization of international relations and the rejection of racism, provides four interlocking elements for social involvement. [20]

2.2.3: Section III, "Spirit of Unity — Reconcile your People!" [21]

As the title suggests, this section provided a theological consideration of the theme of reconciliation. There was a strong stress on reconciliation *between* the churches, but the report also covered wider dimensions, such as reconciliation in a political context and with people of other faiths and ideologies. The report focuses on "ecumenical perspectives on ecclesiology" and "koinonia and unity". Ecclesiological considerations on "community of women and men" were also included. [22]

Consideration of "mission in the power of the spirit — the ministry of reconciliation and sharing" began with the formulation of a theology of reconciliation with clear JPIC implications. The reconciled community, and the overcoming of social and economic division are related to Christ's suffering on the cross.[23]

This theological basis is then exemplified in three points on "whole-ness of mission", "the community of sharing" — which reaffirms the "Guidelines for Sharing" (El Escorial 1987) — and "community of cultures".

The section entitled "Spirit of unity and the encounter with peoples of other faiths and ideologies" has a dual stress — that religion should not be used "as a force of division and conflict",[24] and an affirmation of the authenticity of interfaith dialogue[25] and dialogue with ideologies.[26] A particularly important approach towards the analysis of "hidden ideologies" is made, mentioning "patriarchy", "economic materialism", "achievement-oriented individualism", "pluralism, resulting from uncriti-cal affirmation of secularization" and "modernization which aggressively breaks up the liberative cultural values of the two-thirds world".[27] One of the recommendations from this part of the document calls on the WCC immediately to "bring leaders of the Christian, Muslim and Jewish communities together to explore ways of working in co-operation for peace and justice in the present context of the Middle East crisis".[28]

Section III thus mainly concentrated on ecclesiological and mission-related questions, also taking up the theme of dialogue with other faiths and religions. It prominently mentioned the significance of JPIC among its recommendations.

2.2.4: Section IV, "Holy Spirit — Transform and Sanctify Us!"
The central overt reference to JPIC in the section IV report is, interestingly enough, in an ecclesiological context:

> The churches have in the past committed themselves to act together in all those areas where deep differences do not compel them to act separately (Lund 1952). However, they have failed to fulfill this in word and action. Recently, similar commitments have been made at Seoul (JPIC) and with respect to the Decade for the Churches in Solidarity with Women. These must be taken seriously, be formative for the life of all the churches and remain at the centre of the ecumenical agenda.[29]

The focus of the report is on spirituality, stressing that humanity is created in the image of the Trinitarian God.[30] It is a spirituality "rooted in baptism and discipleship".[31] The report continues by outlining "the mystery of the Holy Spirit",[32] "the church as sacrament and sign",[33] and "responding to the Holy Spirit".[34] In this last-named section, the specific link is made between spirituality and the sabbath (taken over from the Jewish faith) and from there, the connection established between the sabbath principle/jubilee year and the need to relieve the international debt burden.[35] The document proceeds through the work of the Holy Spirit moving us towards unity and working in the world, then, finally, the Spirit's "transforming role of the people of God".[36]

In terms of the outworkings of this spirituality in commitment to justice and peace, the report emphasizes "inclusivity"[37] and "siding with minorities and oppressed peoples"[38] as characteristics for the church. With respect to peace witness, the stress is on a spirituality marked by a "peace-oriented life-style, exploring the power of active non-violence, for the transformation of society".[39]

Here, then, in section IV — as in section III — the link between JPIC and spirituality is both explicitly and implicitly made.

2.3: COMMITTEE ON PROGRAMME POLICY[40]

The review of how the main guidelines for WCC work carried forward from Vancouver specifically included "growing towards justice and peace" as one of the five emphases. It was under this heading that JPIC was especially mentioned in this "between the assemblies" context — although mention was also made under (E) of the Seoul Bible study material:

> The Vancouver assembly said that commitment to justice, peace and the wellbeing of the whole creation should be one of the purposes of all programmes of the WCC. In general, sub-units had this aim before them in their programmes. The specific effort made through the JPIC process has served to awaken member churches to the urgency of the issues.
>
> In the last seven years we have seen important movement towards liberation, justice and peace for which we give thanks to God. The WCC's share in inspiring some of these changes has not been insignificant. Periodic actions and public statements, letters from the general secretary, visits to areas of conflict by WCC teams, support to churches and groups in their struggle against poverty, oppression and racism, have all been helpful.[41]

It was in this paper that the future policy directions of the WCC were outlined. The Canberra assembly defined three major areas: (a) unity of the church; (b) justice, peace and the integrity of creation; (c) wholeness of the mission of the church.

In purely quantitative terms the JPIC emphasis post-Canberra is one of three main priority areas, whereas "growing towards justice and peace" was one of five in the Vancouver-Canberra period. If this is taken as significant, it implies a strengthening of the centrality of JPIC. In addition, there are clear indications of JPIC being a thread through the other priority areas as well — thus JPIC is not just one area among three; it is in all three areas, with one specifically entitled JPIC. So, for example under "unity of the church", we read:

> Through our participation in struggles for justice and liberation we share a common unity through solidarity with all of humanity and can become ecumenical in the fullest sense. [42]

This affirmation picks up the 1971 Louvain Faith and Order theme "Unity of the Church and Unity of Mankind" (which would certainly be rephrased if held today, in terms of "unity of humanity" or "humankind"). That was the conference which prompted Ernst Lange's great ecumenical book, *And Yet It Moves...* [43] with his reflections on conciliarity and much more. In many ways, the connection between Faith and Order perspectives and Church and Society issues and approaches was more organic twenty years ago, although the new Faith and Order study *Church and World* [44] specifically takes up the theme again in its subtitle "The Unity of the Church and the Renewal of Human Community".

The JPIC section of the report had been further strengthened (as will be seen below) in a way which, in my view, finds inadequate expression in the version contained in the assembly report. The relevant section in the report reads as follows:

> In this assembly we have realized more intensely that the Holy Spirit lays upon us the task which Jesus himself accepted. The Holy Spirit opens our eyes to see the injustice of the world and strengthens us to resist and struggle against oppression and the devastation of creation. The Holy Spirit calls us to work together towards just social systems and towards a sustainable environment. We seek a world of social and economic justice and care for those who are vulnerable and dispossessed. We seek a world in which all participate in decisions which affect their lives. We seek a world based on the biblical vision of economic and ecological reconciliation. The vision of justice, peace and the integrity of creation needs to become embodied in the realities of our contextual situation. This calls for a broad co-operation with secular groups, between the churches, and with people of other faiths.
>
> We confess that nations which claim to be Christian shoulder a substantial part of the blame for the present global military-industrial-technological civilization insofar as it breeds injustice, foments wars and disrupts the eco-balance.

The struggle for justice, peace and the integrity of creation may entail the questioning of some of the values on which this civilization is based. This vision should enable the WCC to focus on the central ethical concerns of our time.

Working towards justice, peace and the integrity of creation will help the churches understand their task in the world, provided we develop a rigorous social analysis, deepen our theological reflection and vigorously promote these concerns. This has emerged as the central vision of the WCC and its member churches as they face the next assembly when they can give an account of their efforts to fulfill the covenants made for JPIC.

At Vancouver it was assumed that *participation* was implied in the concept of justice, because justice includes participation in power; however, participation in itself has not received the attention it should. Our future work must be based on local, national, regional and inter-regional contexts. We need to intensify and deepen concrete analysis of the root causes and institutional structures of injustice. Inter-racial, inter-regional and multicultural interaction is essential to new understanding and action without domination of one culture over the other. [45]

In the plenary debate on the report, which was interrupted by an overnight break (19-20 February), towards the close of business on the first day of the debate, an amendment giving clearer commitment to the future work of JPIC within the Council and reaffirming the 1990 central committee decisions was presented by Margot Kässmann (EKD, Germany). The amendment fell into two parts. The first part was simply to strengthen statements in section IV.B of the report. The text follows, with the original wording in italics and the Kässmann proposal in brackets:

> The struggle for justice, peace and the integrity of creation *may*/(does) entail the questioning of some of the values on which this civilization is based.
>
> Working towards justice, peace and the integrity of creation *could*/(will) help the churches understand their task in the world, provided we develop a rigorous social analysis and deepen our theological reflection. [46]

The former change does not appear in the assembly report but the latter does. [47]

The second and more substantive part of Kässmann's amendment was initially considered to be an alternative to paragraphs VI.B and C, but was later proposed as an *addition* to para VI.B in the section entitled "VI. Programme policies that should undergird and inspire all WCC programmes in the coming years". The proposed text by Kässmann read:

> We agree with the WCC central committee meeting of 1990 in stating that the process for JPIC is at the heart of the ecumenical vision for the next

millennium. This process is the perspective from which the WCC in future times has to discuss the central ethical concerns of our time. The WCC should be the connecting body between initiatives for JPIC in the member churches and provide impetus to this process. [48]

Time did not permit this amendment, which had been moved formally, to be voted upon. During the recess, the mover of the amendment was informed by Soritua Nababan (Batak Protestant Christian Church, Indonesia), as moderator of the Committee, that the amendment was acceptable to the Committee. It therefore became unnecessary to vote upon the amendment when business resumed, since the amendment now became part of the substantive motion, with the Committee's support. Thus, when the paper was formally approved by the plenary, this amendment was part of the paper agreed. It therefore comes as a surprise to those who have followed the process of discussion carefully that the final text as given in the assembly report omits this text approved by the assembly, and that the WCC subsequently circulated the weaker and less binding version cited above — which has a less concrete organizational commitment than the Kässmann text, especially when the 1990 central committee decision calling for the establishment of a JPIC centre of exchange is included. Correspondence to the author from deputy general secretary Mercy Amba Oduyoye states that there is no intention to water down the commitment on JPIC and that the relevant committee at Canberra took the decision as involving the intention rather than the specific verbatim wording of Kässmann's proposal. [49]

The only concessions in the direction of the Kässmann amendment were the addition of the following sentence to one paragraph of IV.B: "This vision should enable the WCC to focus on the central ethical concerns of our time" and the rewording of a further paragraph of IV.B as follows (italic text):

> Working towards justice, peace and the integrity of creation will help the churches understand their task in the world, provided we develop a rigorous social analysis, deepen our theological reflection and vigorously promote these concerns. *This has emerged as the central vision of the WCC and its member churches as they face the next assembly when they can give an account of their efforts to fulfill the covenants made for JPIC.*

The sentence in italics replaced the following from the previous version:

> This can be a central vision of the WCC and its member churches as they face the next assembly when they can give an account of their efforts to fulfill the covenants made for JPIC.

In my view, even the strengthening which did occur (e.g. from "*a* central vision" to "*the* central vision") hardly covers the substance of the more comprehensive amendment which was actually approved. In any case, the clear recommendation of the 1990 central committee still holds — the more so since it was specifically reaffirmed in Canberra.

The section on future programme policies outlined five ways in which the three thematic foci (unity, JPIC and wholeness) could be made more concrete. Some short comments are required on each sub-theme:

A. Renewal through reconciliation: The significance of JPIC is specifically stressed:

> Dialogue with people of other faiths must continue to be promoted, particularly for co-operation in our common quest for justice, peace and the integrity of creation. Such dialogue is urgent in situations throughout the world where religious communities are divided by fear and mistrust.[50]

The last sentence was added as a result of plenary discussion on the draft.

B. Renewal through freedom and justice: Freedom is stressed as a "gift of the Spirit". In the power of the Spirit we must confront injustice "be it economic or political, cultural or social, of gender, race or ecology" (this last point is distinctly odd — surely it is a misreading for "ideology" which survived through the editorial process). Once more JPIC is specifically affirmed: "The issues of justice, peace and the integrity of creation provide us with an effective framework for accomplishing these goals."[51]

C. Renewal through right relationship with the creation: Theology of creation has emerged as a strong JPIC theme during the Vancouver-Canberra period. The precursors for such an ecological approach include Joseph Sittler's New Delhi 1961 speech which stressed salvation as a cosmic process (based on Col. 1:15-20)[52] and Charles Birch's Nairobi 1975 speech, warning that, in ecological terms "the world is a Titanic on a collision course".[53] The linking of the struggle of indigenous peoples, land rights, indigenous spirituality and the theology of creation comes out more clearly in this assembly than previously.

D. Renewal through enabling the full participation and contribution of women: This passage was strengthened as a result of the plenary debate, with an added insistence on the goal of *visible unity* in the building of a *renewed* community of women and men (emphasis to show additions as a result of plenary discussion). The Decade of the Churches in Solidarity with Women is strongly stressed.[54]

E. Renewal through an ecumenical spirituality for our times: The final point focuses on a theology of the cross, the need for service and "the significance of Christian life-style, of holiness, of a spirituality of non-violence, common prayer, liturgical life, asceticism and sharing".[55]

Taken together with the affirmation of JPIC as one of the three major themes for WCC work after the assembly, these attempts to make more concrete the future programme of the WCC show that the emphasis on JPIC concerns must feed into all programme areas of the WCC's work. Furthermore, the need for inter-relationship between the issues, the connection between spirituality and action and joint efforts with people of other faiths (so far an underdeveloped dimension of JPIC) came through strongly in Canberra in the programme policy document.

3. Future perspectives

It is not the place or purpose of this document to comment on the detailed structure required for the WCC in coming years. However, the very clear message from the Canberra assembly is that JPIC has proved a promising organizing and co-ordinating principle for action and reflection in the Vancouver-Canberra period. The assembly stated in many different ways that JPIC must be continued, deepened, broadened, conducted with greater energy, and so on.

Certain themes emerged strongly from the assembly: gospel and culture (inculturation); the search for visible unity; JPIC; the continued need for a vital and coherent theology, as well as the stress on sharing; and reconciliation and dialogue with other faiths. The assembly was equally firm in maintaining that JPIC is both an area of vital importance *and* a dimension for all future programmes. Thus, JPIC is:[56]

a) an instrument for unity — cf. the section IV report in particular mentions the ecclesiological significance of JPIC in a paragraph linking JPIC with the Lund formula (cited above);[57]

b) an instrument for mission — see the section III report;[58]

c) an approach for dialogue and joint action with people of other faiths — stressed in the section III report;[59]

d) a key to future ecumenical theological work — JPIC could, according to the programme policy report, "help the churches understand their task in the world, provided we develop a rigorous social analysis, deepen our theological reflection and vigorously promote these concerns";[60]

e) a framework for promoting renewal — "a reconciled and renewed creation is the goal of the mission of the church. This mission requires that the search for the sacramental communion of the church be more closely linked with the struggle for justice and peace."[61]

In addition to these, one also needs to add that JPIC is:

f) an impulse towards regional and inter-regional co-operation: "Regional solidarity in the peace work of the churches must be strengthened."[62]

4. JPIC must go on!

The Seoul convocation agreed on the following strong statement concerning the act of covenanting and concretizations on economic justice, demilitarization of international relations, protection of the atmosphere and opposition to racism:

> As participants in the world convocation on "Justice, Peace and the Integrity of Creation" meeting in Seoul, March 1990, we covenant together on the four areas that follow, and commit ourselves to raise them (and the practical issues of application which follow from them) within our churches, and to report on progress to the seventh assembly of the World Council of Churches in February 1991.[63]

This reporting has not happened in any systematic way as yet, for two reasons. First, the deadline set was too short, given the major task of preparation for the assembly. Secondly, the WCC so far has not organized this process of reporting on progress in a comprehensive and energetic way. This remains a task to be conducted in the next phase of the JPIC process. There are many other tasks which indicate that specific staff will need to be allocated to this work (either full-time as JPIC staff or part-time within departments) — tasks such as relating to the emphasis on co-ordination of peace efforts, lay training and involvement and inter-regional participation.

In addition, the major work called for on JPIC in relation to other faiths and ideologies is in itself an important result of the assembly's deliberations. Such tasks require the reorganization of the WCC into a structure that puts JPIC at the heart of the ecumenical movement — together with the search for a vital and coherent theology. This requires a strong staffing commitment to the distinctive programmatic thrusts of JPIC as outlined in the ten affirmations and the four concretizations of the Seoul covenant. It would not be an adequate response to allow the JPIC office in its pre-assembly form to disappear, and to point to activities called for in one or other of the affirmations and argue: "JPIC continues — affirmation one is covered here, affirmation seven is done over there." This would be to divide up again what, many would argue, God put together. The JPIC process has been one of the few WCC programmes with a genuine grassroots constituency, which has united the oikoumene as ecumenical *movement* and as institution of the churches. To slice up JPIC into sub-unit-sized chunks and lose the cross-connections which have proved so fruitful would be an immense mistake.

During the assembly, an informal group met on an ad hoc basis to report to one another on progress concerning JPIC in the various sections. It was a representative group involving about forty participants at various times, mainly delegates, but with advisers and staff also involved. Most members of the group worked in one of the first three sections. It was geographically representative, with persons known to be active on JPIC concerns from the various world regions. This group wrote, discussed and rewrote a paper which was eventually submitted to the Programme Policy Committee as a recommendation.

Many of the aspects of this paper on "JPIC and the Threats to Life" are reflected in the documents of the assembly. Passages from "JPIC and the Threats to Life" provide a clear summary of what has been achieved and what needs to be done. For reasons of space only the sections dealing with future programme are cited and a verdict given on the basis of the assembly documents how far the call has been met:

Future work and programme needs
— JPIC should be strengthened and developed as a main programme emphasis following the Canberra assembly.
— While the restructuring of the WCC is being discussed, an interim arrangement is required. A JPIC centre of exchange should be established immediately after the assembly in order to maintain the momentum of JPIC (see central committee resolution 1990 which requires this level of response). (From "JPIC and the Threats to Life", part three.)

The proposed functions of such a centre are listed below, immediately followed by reference to the assembly documents.
a) *networking between churches and church agencies, movements and action groups:* "Regional solidarity in the peace work of the churches must be strengthened" (section II, issue 5, recommendations to the churches 1, p.88);
b) *work on practical implementation of JPIC, e.g. operationalizing commitments to the affirmations and covenant;*
c) *continued ecumenical work, in particular with the Roman Catholic Church:* "It is evident that the Holy Spirit has been active in strengthening the relationships between the Roman Catholic Church and the national and regional councils of churches. The Basel assembly (1989) organized by a regional council of churches and the

regional episcopal conference might provide a useful model of co-operation" (section 4, 5.33, p.116);[64]

d) *encouraging regional and inter-regional encounters on the JPIC issues (e.g. Latin America-Europe on 1992 — 500th anniversary of the colonial era beginning):* "Our future work must be based on local, national, regional and inter-regional contexts. We need to intensify and deepen concrete analysis of the root causes and institutional structures of injustice" (programme policy, IV.B, p.187). On the 500th anniversary of Columbus's arrival in Latin America, see section II, issue 3, recommendation 7, p.82. Section II also notes 1992 as an example of a "common theme" running through the section's entire work (section II, "Common themes" 3, p.93);

e) *attention to the interfaith dimensions of dialogue and action. JPIC provides an ideal framework for interfaith dialogue and joint action:* See "Reconciliation with people of other faiths", Section III, C.1, pp.104-5;

f) *unmasking destructive ideologies and the formulation of positive alternatives:* See section on "hidden ideologies" mentioned above in discussion of the section III report;

g) *opposition to distorted communication and media misrepresentation of JPIC concerns:* See "The challenge of communication for liberation", section II, issue 4, pp.83-85;

h) *deepening theological perspectives on the JPIC process (interconnections, covenanting and the binding character of the process):* "The challenge... is for... the WCC to call all churches... to re-commit themselves to work for justice, peace and the integrity of creation, linking more closely the search for the sacramental communion of the church with the struggles for justice and peace" ("The Unity of the Church as Koinonia: Gift and Calling", 3.2. p.174; quoted in full in the report of the Reference Committee, emerging from discussions in section III, cf. p.98.);

i) *study and reflection on the subject matter of JPIC (e.g. debt crisis, biotechnology, paths to demilitarization etc.):* This is a recurrent theme in sections I and II in particular;

j) *strengthening, developing and promoting the Seoul covenant:* "The churches should commit themselves to the affirmations of the Seoul convocation.... The Seoul covenant... provides four interlocking elements for social involvement" (section II, issue 5, pp.87-8).

Thus each of the requirements outlined found backing in the Canberra final documents.

Longer-term perspectives

The above issues, initially the subject matter for the centre of exchange, can be carried on effectively on a longer-term basis only if the reorganization of the WCC has JPIC at the centre of its ecumenical vision, as the 1990 central committee meeting already clearly affirmed.

• The year 1998, a prospective date for the next assembly, should be a *time of accounting* concerning JPIC for the churches. The call was issued by the WCC at Vancouver. The churches are active and must have an opportunity to give witness to their efforts to fulfill this serious commitment.

• As the fiftieth anniversary of the first WCC assembly, it should be a time when the challenge of *jubilee* is addressed with particular urgency to economic justice (an appropriate response to the debt crisis).

• It should be a time of accounting where churches indicate what they have done for JPIC, how the ten affirmations and four parts of the covenant have been implemented within their life.

• It should provide a time of accounting for the full integration of JPIC into the life of the churches through the Ecumenical Decade of the Churches in Solidarity with Women.

• JPIC further requires intensified lay training, leadership formation, ecumenical learning and youth activities.

• It should give the basis for the liberative "wider ecumenism" of solidarity with all who are acting in defence of the "whole inhabited earth". (From "JPIC and the Threats to Life", part four)

Assembly verdict: The challenge was taken up in the amendment put to the programme policy document by Margot Kässmann (see above). It is still to be found in the document in a weaker form — and full implementation of the 1990 central committee resolution is still outstanding.

Jubilee and sabbath: "The sabbath principle serves as a protection against unlimited activity and unrelenting desire for profit. The sabbath-year, once in fifty years, was intended to break the spiral by which the rich became richer and the poor poorer (Lev. 25:8-17). It is relevant to apply this in the debt-ridden parts of the international community. The burden of debts should be lifted and the world economic order revised in favour of the poor" (section 4, 4.22, p.114). See also "Towards an Ethic of Economy and Ecology: A Vision" (section I, pp.59-60).

The next assembly as a time of accounting: "This [referring to JPIC] has emerged as the central vision of the WCC and its member churches as they face the next assembly when they can give an account of their efforts to fulfill the covenants made for JPIC" (Programme Policy, IV.B, p.187).

The Ecumenical Decade of the Churches in Solidarity with Women: See "Issue Six: Justice for Women", section II, pp.89-91. Section III also takes up the issue in its recommendations (section III.A, recommendations, p.99).

Lay training, etc.: "Lay training, leadership formation and ecumenical learning must be strengthened as a key instrument to promote many WCC priorities especially JPIC" (section II, issue 5, recommendations to the churches, no. 3, p.88).

Liberative wider ecumenism: "A reconciled and renewed creation is the goal of the mission of the church. The vision of God uniting all things in Christ is the driving force of its life and sharing. Sharing also means that we work concretely to overcome economic disparities and social antagonisms between classes, castes, races, sexes and cultures. The diversity of cultures is of immediate relevance to the church's ministry of reconciliation and sharing for it affects both the relationships within churches and also the relationship with people of other faiths" (section III.B, p.100). [65]

5. Final verdict

There is thus more than enough support for such a far-reaching conclusion in the results of the Canberra assembly. The decision based on a careful reading of the section reports and other assembly documents must therefore be — "JPIC must go on!" To return to our title, there is no reason for putting asunder what has so fruitfully been brought together in the ecumenical process for justice, peace and the integrity of creation.

NOTES

[1] "Report of Reference Committee", para. 3., *Signs of the Spirit*, official report of the WCC's seventh assembly, M. Kinnamon ed., Geneva, WCC, 1991 (hereafter referred to as WCC assembly report), p.170.

[2] "Central Place of Humans Questioned", in *Assembly Line*, no. 7, 15.2.1991, p.1.

[3] Section I report — final version "Giver of Life — Sustain your Creation!", WCC assembly report, pp.54-71. Quote from para. 15, p.58.

[4] *Ibid.*, para. 37, pp.64-65, & para. 63, p.69.

[5] *Ibid.*, para. 33, pp.63-64.

[6] *Ibid.*, paras 47-73, pp.67-71.

[7] *Ibid.*, para. 52, p.67.

[8] *Ibid.*, para. 62, p.69.

[9] *Ibid.*, para. 64, p.69.

[10] *Ibid.*, both quotes from para. 67, p.70.

[11] Section II final report, "Spirit of Truth — Set us Free!", WCC assembly report, pp.73-93. Quote from "Issue one: The challenge to be free in order to struggle", issue one, recommendation 1, p.75.

[12] *Ibid.*, issue one, recommendation 3, p.75.

[13] *Ibid.*, "Issue two: The challenge to evolve a sustainable value system", pp.76-79.

[14] *Ibid.*, "Issue three: The challenge to work for racial justice", recommendation 1, p.82.

[15] *Ibid.*, "Issue five: The challenge for lasting peace and meaningful security", p.87. The points referred to do not appear anywhere in the document of the programme policy committee. They were removed from the section II report primarily because of clear instructions that only two pages of text would be entertained from each of the groups working on their particular issue. Thus detail and specificity in the recommendations have been lost to the official record of the assembly. At this point, the text from Seoul is fuller and better.

[16] *Ibid.*, "Issue five: Recommendations to the churches", p.88.

[17] *Ibid.*, "Recommendations for the WCC", pp.88-89.

[18] Quoted in: "Churches must redress injustice", in *Assembly Line*, no. 11, 20.2.1991, p.1.

[19] WCC assembly report, section II report: "III. Common themes", pp.92-93.

[20] *Ibid.*, issue five, pp.87-88.

[21] WCC assembly report, section III report, pp.96-111.

[22] *Ibid.*, recommendation 5, p.99.

[23] Cf. *ibid.*, part B., pp.100-103.

[24] *Ibid.*, C.1., p.104.

[25] *Ibid.*

[26] *Ibid.*, C.2., pp.105-106.

[27] *Ibid.*, part C.2., p.106.

[28] *Ibid.*, p.107.

[29] WCC assembly report, section IV report "Holy Spirit — Transform and Sanctify Us!", para. 34, p.116.

[30] *Ibid.*, para. 1.3, p.111.

[31] *Ibid.*, para. 1.5, p.112.

[32] *Ibid.*, section 2, p.112.

[33] *Ibid.*, part 3, p.113.

[34] *Ibid.*, part 4, pp.113-5.

[35] *Ibid.*, paras. 4.21 & 4.22, p.114.

[36] *Ibid.*, parts 5,6,7 respectively, pp.115-117.

[37] *Ibid.*, part 8, pp.117-118.

[38] *Ibid.*, para. 8.46, p.118.

[39] *Ibid.*, para. 9.47, p.118.

[40] WCC assembly report, "Report of the Programme Policy Committee", pp.183-192.

[41] *Ibid.*, section III.B, p.184-185.

[42] *Ibid.*, IV.A, p.186.

[43] E. Lange, *And Yet It Moves… Dream and Reality of the Ecumenical Movement*, Grand Rapids, Eerdmans, 1979.

[44] *Church and World: The Unity of the Church and the Renewal of Human Community*, Faith and Order Paper no. 151, Geneva, WCC, 1990.

[45] "Report of the Programme Policy Committee", section IV.B, pp.186-187.

[46] *Ibid.*

[47] WCC assembly report, p.187.

[48] Handwritten original of wording from Rev. Dr Kässmann.

[49] Letter from Mercy Amba Oduyoye, 26.7.1991.

[50] "Programme Policy", VI.A, p.191.

[51] Quotes from: *ibid.*, VI.B. p.191.

[52] Cf. e.g. K. Slack, *Despatch from New Delhi*, London, SCM, 1962, pp.86-87.

[53] K. Slack, *Nairobi Narrative*, London, SCM, 1976, pp.55-57.

[54] "Programme Policy", VI.D, p.192.

[55] *Ibid.*, VI.E, p.192.

[56] Headings for these points emerge from the internal WCC staff evaluation. The illustration from assembly documents is my own.

[57] Section IV report, 5.34, p.116.

[58] Cf. Section III report, part B, pp.100-103 (cited above in note 23).

[59] "Reconciliation with people of other faiths", in section III report, C.1, pp.104-105.

[60] "Programme Policy", IV.B. p.187.

[61] *Ibid.*, IV.C, p.187.

[62] Section II, issue five, recommendations to the churches no. 1, p.88.

[63] *Now Is the Time: Final Document and Other Texts: World Convocation on Justice, Peace and the Integrity of Creation, Seoul 1990*, Geneva, WCC, 1990, section 2.3.2., p.24.

[64] The Catholic partner was actually the Council of European Bishops' Conferences, which is not technically speaking a regional episcopal conference.

[65] On the need for a wider liberative ecumenism between the faiths, cf. "The EATWOT Consultation on Religion and Liberation, New Delhi, 1-5 December 1987", in *The Ecumenical Review*, vol. 41, no. 1, January 1989, pp.117-24.

Catholic Social Teaching and Ecumenical Social Ethics

René Coste

For an ecumenical social ethics

At Canberra the moderator of the central committee appealed in particularly well-chosen terms for effort to be devoted to working out a common social ethics:

> More work must be done on a common theological understanding of creation and on an ecumenical social ethics which takes account of the questions of human survival that are being asked, even beyond the relatively narrow circle of our member churches.[1]

Is it not a fundamental requirement of our faith to contribute to transforming society in the light of the gospel, as section IV put it so well?

The position taken by the Programme Policy Committee should meet with unanimous assent:

> The Holy Spirit calls us to work together towards just social systems and towards a sustainable environment. We seek a world in which all can participate in decisions which affect their lives. We seek a world based on the biblical vision of economic and ecological reconciliation. The vision of justice, peace and the integrity of creation needs to become embodied in the realities of our contextual situation.[2]

• This text was translated from the French by the WCC Language Service.

The aim of working out an ecumenical social ethic is manifestly shared by the Roman Catholic Church. It is necessarily implied in its desire for economic co-operation as expounded by Vatican II:

> Such co-operation, which has already begun in many countries, should be developed more and more, particularly in regions where social and technological evolution is taking place. It should contribute to a just appreciation of the dignity of the human person, to the promotion of the blessings of peace, the application of the principles of the gospel to social life... It should use every possible means to relieve the afflictions of our times, such as famine and natural disasters, illiteracy and poverty, lack of housing and the unequal distribution of wealth.[3]

It is also implied in the following position adopted by John Paul II, referring explicitly to the JPIC process:

> The present tragic situation of our troubled world confirms once again humanity's need for reconciliation, its need for an ever more authentic witness to the biblical message of peace, justice and the integrity of creation.[4]

The constant concern of Catholic social teaching has been well-known since Leo XIII: to contribute actively to working out a universal ethic which could be recognized by all humanity, even non-believers — at least through the acceptance of certain fundamental criteria (an aim which since then has become essential for the future of our planet). How could the Roman Catholic Church possibly fail to want even more a common ethical purpose among all the Christians in the world? As Roman Catholic social teaching since Vatican II — more precisely since the Pastoral Constitution on the Church in the World Today — has been given a strong biblical foundation,[5] while maintaining concern for a process of thought that might be accepted by non-Christians, this ought greatly to facilitate the ecumenical process.

The problem of divergences

It is perfectly true that serious divergences still exist, as is noted in the sixth report of the Joint Working Group between the Roman Catholic Church and the World Council of Churches. After noting that all "Christian traditions recognize that ethics cannot be separated from revealed doctrine: faith does have ethical consequences", it goes on: "... in fact there is not enough serious, mature and sustained ecumenical discussion on many of these ethical issues and positions, personal and social: for example, nuclear armaments and deterrence, abortion and euthanasia, permanent married love and procreation, genetic engineering and artificial insemination". It fears that new ecumenical divisions may result from this, and proposes that these ethical problems should "be a priority for the post-Canberra period".[6]

I shall give only one example. The sixth assembly of the WCC denied any ethical legitimacy to nuclear deterrence, whereas John Paul II in his message of 11 June 1982 to the second special session of the General Assembly of the United Nations on disarmament saw the deterrent as "morally acceptable" although under strict conditions — as a lesser evil in the international situation at that time, and provided everything is done to find a way out of the tragic impasse in which humanity has incautiously become involved.

Is it enough simply to describe this divergence in outline? Certainly not. To grasp its significance correctly we must place John Paul II's position in the total context of Catholic doctrine on problems of war and peace. On this I take the liberty of referring to two of my articles.[7]

Could the divergences perhaps be insurmountable?

First of all I would point out that the divisions do not appear only in the relations between the churches but are also to be found within the churches.

Then I would observe that the common ground between Catholic social ethics and that of the ecumenical bodies is already considerable. We may see it, for example, when we read the final document of the European Ecumenical Assembly in Basel. It may also be noted that the social encyclicals of John Paul II have generally been well received in ecumenical circles. The divergences must not blind us to the existence of fundamental convergences.

Everything leads one to think that rigorous theological work, taking into account scientific analyses of life and society, ought to reduce the divergences and even cause some of them to disappear.

For its part, too, Roman Catholic social teaching deliberately assumes the interconnection of "justice, peace and the integrity of creation"

As a Catholic theologian I am happy to recognize the pioneering role played in this field by the ecumenical dynamic of "justice, peace and the integrity of creation".[8] Catholic doctrine has always paid attention to the interconnection of peace and justice. It is more than twenty years since it began to include with these the third of the three terms.

I shall mention at least a few major papal documents.

First, the excellent message from Paul VI to the United Nations Conference on the Environment (Stockholm, 5-17 June 1972) and the high quality work carried out there by the delegation from the holy see; then the address of John Paul II to the United Nations Centre at Nairobi on 18 August 1985, in which we read this theological statement: "The church's care for the conservation and improvement of our environment is bound up with God's command"; thirdly the tribute paid to "ecological concern" (the literal expression) in the encyclical Sollicitudo Rei Socialis of 30 December 1987; fourthly, the message from John Paul II in celebration of the World Day of Peace, 1 January 1990, splendidly entitled "Peace with God the Creator, Peace with all Creation". The following comment deserves to be kept in mind: "A just environmental balance will not be attained unless we do tackle directly the structural forms of poverty that exist in the world" (no. 11). Finally, the encyclical Centesimus Annus, in which, in regard to environmental matters, John Paul II commends a "disinterested, unselfish and aesthetic attitude that is born of wonder in the presence of being and of the beauty that enables one to see in visible things the message of the invisible God who created them" (no. 37). In it he also calls for the safeguarding of the *moral conditions for an authentic "human ecology"*: in particular for the promotion of urban planning which is concerned with how people are to live, of a *social ecology* of work (no. 38) and furthermore of the family founded on marriage which requires us to "go back to seeing the family as the *sanctuary of life*" (no. 39).

A number of bishops' conferences have shown the same concern.

The Basel, Seoul and Canberra experiences

As a Catholic theologian I was actively involved in the Basel, Seoul and Canberra assemblies. At Basel, as a member of the preparatory group and of the committee editing the final document; at Seoul as a member of the preparatory group of the delegation from the holy see; at Canberra as an adviser of the delegation from the holy see. My experience of the three assemblies enables me to attempt to evaluate them briefly with regard to the working out of an ecumenical social ethics.

A. The convergence between Catholic social ethics and the social ethics of the final document from Basel is, all in all, remarkable. It is true that the Catholic church took part in it as a full member, and above all in the preparatory group and the editorial committee. Such a positive result is due to the excellent dialogue that constantly prevailed there.[9]

It is not without interest to note (with reference to the problem of nuclear deterrence raised above) that "the system of nuclear deterrence [would have to be] overcome and be replaced by a different, less dangerous system of security" (no. 86 c). Quite clearly the editors wanted to leave on one side — but in no way forgetting it — the serious ethical debate that divides the churches on this matter, whether to condemn it outright or to tolerate it for the time being under strict conditions. What they rightly wanted to highlight — and what won the agreement of the Basel assembly — was that despite this disagreement (which there is no question at all of playing down), there does exist an ecumenical consensus that the deterrent is not an appropriate strategy for guaranteeing peace long-term, and that contrary to its many (political and military) supporters we must work actively to create conditions which make it possible to get beyond the policy of deterrence in a genuine peace process. The ecumenical consensus in fact agrees on the need to give urgent priority to this matter.

I shall also recall this statement of the final document: that it is "essential that the vital concerns for justice, peace and the integrity of creation should not be separated from the mission of the church to proclaim the gospel" (no. 79). This is to affirm in a minor key what we find stated with impressive forcefulness in several official documents of the Catholic church such as, for example, *Justice in the World* by the Synod of Bishops (1971), the apostolic exhortation Evangelii Nuntiandi of Paul VI, and the encyclicals Sollicitudo Rei Socialis and Centesimus Annus of John Paul II. The highlighting of the social dimension of the Christian faith is one of the great novelties of theology and pastoralia in our day. On this matter it is possible to speak of an ecumenical consensus.

B. It is well-known that the theological results from Seoul were manifestly less happy — to a significant degree, because the preparatory group did not manage to achieve the theological co-operation that would have been desirable. It is true that this was more difficult to do at the global level than at the European continental level.

As a theologian I am happy to go along with the headings of the ten theological affirmations of the convocation. And I also accept most of their explications. Passages here and there would have merited re-working.

I am particularly happy about the adoption of the "preferential option for the poor".

In relation to two of the problems given most attention at Seoul I shall recall two major documents of the Pontifical Commission on "Justice and

Peace": *Serving the Human Community: an Ethical Approach to Foreign Debt* (1986), and *The Church and Racism* (1988).

At Canberra far too many ethical problems were brought up to make it possible to tackle any one of them in depth. However, some significant appeals were stated there, which were of prime importance for working out an ecumenical social ethics. First of all that this is a necessity — which I have already mentioned; also, that it is essential to deepen the theology of the Holy Spirit and to have critical discernment, and also the appeal regarding the continuation of research on a theology of creation. The emphasis placed on *communion* (koinonia) as a central ecclesiological concept, both by section IV and by the moderator of the central committee, is also of great significance. The latter's statement of this is one of the best I know. [10]

Points made by John Paul II on Catholic social teaching

So that dialogue and co-operation can develop it is necessary both for Catholic theologians to have a good knowledge of the practice of ecumenical bodies in the field of social ethics, and for other Christian theologians to be conversant with the evolution of ideas on Catholic social teaching — in particular, John Paul's conception of what it is.

It is necessary to know that for him — as he explains in the encyclical Sollicitudo Rei Socialis — the social doctrine of the church has become "an updated doctrinal 'corpus'. It builds up gradually, as the church in the fullness of the word revealed by Christ Jesus and with the assistance of the Holy Spirit... reads events as they unfold in the course of history" (no. 1). He shows clearly the need to reaffirm its continuity... as well as its constant renewal (no. 3). He recalls that the church does not have technical solutions to offer for the problem of underdevelopment as such (no. 41); application of a general principle to this specific problem which was that of the encyclical. The statement is to be interpreted open-endedly, for the encyclical itself does not refrain from suggesting certain principles as guidelines which are particularly important from the "technical" standpoint — such as reform of the international trading system or the international monetary and financial system. Clearly these proposals must have a solid basis. The reservation of the Catholic church in relation to "technical solutions" stems from its desire to respect the specific fields of competence of the various social authorities and the liberty of Christians.

For John Paul II the social teaching of the church is not a *third way*, neither is it an *ideology*. It constitutes *a category of its own*. He stresses that it belongs to the field, not of ideology, but of theology and particularly moral theology. He is not afraid to state that the teaching and spreading of its social doctrine are part of the church's evangelizing mission, and he adds this significant point: the condemnation of evils and injustices is also part of that ministry of evangelization in the social field which is an aspect of the church's prophetic role. But it should be made clear that proclamation is always more important than condemnation, and the latter cannot ignore the former, which gives it true solidity and the force of higher motivation (no. 41).

Might we not hope for methodological research in ecumenical social ethics which would take these stances as its starting point?[11] I am convinced that despite the ecclesiological divergences and the differences in theological processes it would be possible to arrive at a consensus on some essential points.

Proposals for common progress

The fundamental problem is methodological. What is needed is a sufficiently well-founded theology that may seem acceptable to all the great Christian traditions (the Basel experience shows it is possible). We also need an objective analysis of the realities — one which can be recognized as valid by well-informed observers. Further work must also be done on the relations to be established between the social sciences, ideologies, ethics, theology and the commitments of the churches and of Christians themselves. How are these commitments to be linked to the word of God which, while enlightening us fundamentally, directs us back to our responsibility? And what is the distinctive mission of the churches in relation to life in society? Moreover, an ecclesial assembly (such as an ecumenical assembly ought to be) must not be a political assembly, even if it aims at having a political impact.

From this standpoint I think it is desirable — in particular — to organize a world ecumenical consultation of a scientific nature which would make every effort to take into account most seriously these fundamental methodological problems (relying moreover on previous research by the churches and the World Council). Preparation for this will itself have to be fully ecumenical, for the choice of themes and speakers is of fundamental importance.

No doubt it would have to be preceded by "regional" consultations (at continental or sub-continental levels) embracing all the above features. On the European level, because of the excellent organization and cordial co-operation developing there out of the JPIC process, such a consultation would be assured of success.

NOTES

[1] Michael Kinnamon ed., *Signs of the Spirit*, official report of the WCC's seventh assembly, Canberra, 1991, Geneva, WCC, 1991, p.138.

[2] *Op. cit.*, p.187.

[3] Unitatis Redintegratio (Decree on Ecumenism), Vatican, no. 12.

[4] Message to the seventh assembly of the WCC, *Signs of the Spirit, op. cit.*, pp.269f.

[5] Cf. especially John Paul II's encyclicals.

[6] Joint Working Group Sixth Report, Geneva-Rome, 1990, p.5.

[7] "Un concile de la paix de toutes les Eglises chrétiennes et l'Eglise catholique aujour-d'hui?", in *Esprit et vie*, 1985, pp.17-24; "La doctrine de la paix de Jean-Paul II", in *Esprit et vie*, 1989, pp.593-605, 609-616.

[8] Cf. R. Coste, *Paix, Justice, Gérance de la Création*, Paris, Nouvelle Cité, 1989; R. Coste & J.P. Ribaut, *Sauvegarde et gérance de la création*, Paris, Desclée, 1991.

[9] Cf. my article "Paix et justice pour la création entière", "Le rassemblement oecuménique européen de Bâle", in *Documents-Episcopat*, 1 January 1990.

[10] *Signs of the Spirit, op. cit.*, p.139. See also my article, "Théologie de l'Esprit saint et notre responsabilité chrétienne aujourd'hui. Brèves réflexions à propos de la Septième assemblée du Conseil oecuménique des Eglises", in *Esprit et vie*, 1992, pp.145-152.

[11] Cf. my article "Sciences sociales, idéologies, éthique, théologie et doctrine sociale dans l'encyclique *Sollicitudo Rei Socialis*", in *Esprit et vie*, 1990, pp.104-112.

New Challenges, Visions and Signs of Hope
Orthodox Insights on JPIC

Gennadios Limouris

Since the Vancouver assembly in 1983 the attention of the World Council of Churches has been focused on "Justice, Peace and the Integrity of Creation", a conciliar process which has stimulated discussion on the unity of the church and challenged theologians and the WCC member and non-member churches, including the Roman Catholic Church, to take their own stand on this issue.

This promising development, however, displays some drawbacks. The discussion of the meaning of creation and its integrity and of the meaning of covenant, "the conciliar process of mutual commitment",[1] and its doctrinal and social understanding in our times, is largely conditioned by the teachings and traditions of individual churches and marked by dogmatism rather than dialogue.

The JPIC discussion during the last five years has seriously suffered from this. It was not surprising that the Seoul convocation in 1990 was unable to reach any ecumenical consensus.

In spite of the promising development at the Vancouver assembly and the encouragement and endorsement of Canberra (1991), JPIC has not yet yielded an integrated discussion concerning the issues of the theology of creation (conducted mainly under Church and Society auspices) and the theology of the sacraments (taking place exclusively within Faith and Order). Thus not much has been achieved even regarding the expectation that the ecumenical agreement in the areas of baptism, eucharist and ministry would also bear fruit within a broader discussion among the faithful about the problems confronting them in their daily life and work. In this respect it is striking that in the joint consultation on creation (Dublin, 1988) an attempt was in fact made to establish a relation between the JPIC programme and the Faith and Order study project on "Confessing the One Faith",[2] but unfortunately there has been no follow-up or further collaboration.[3]

The conversations at Seoul, as well as its main results, have been criticized not only by Orthodox participants but also by Protestant theologians. There was a general feeling that the convocation was not well prepared; that Seoul's theology was irrelevant and its resolutions, reflections and affirmations were mainly based on the horizontal secularized ethic of classical humanism.

Perhaps the theologians will have to do better, as Nietzsche used to say. In the Tradition of the church they will find adequate material, but then about which Tradition are we talking?

It must be affirmed, however, that the justice of God calls for a word from the church. Only the church can give a soul to economic development, and development can serve spiritual values as well. As Berdyaev, the Russian philosopher, used to say: "Bread for me is a material question, bread for my neighbour is a spiritual question."

Hence the Orthodox contribution to and their task in the JPIC process was to draw a social ecclesiology from the biblical tradition and the church fathers, and to try to theologize on these areas through its lived and experienced ecclesial life.[4]

The church of Christ, being not of this world but abiding *in* and *for* the world, cannot remain outside world events and be indifferent[5] to the tragic situations and to the ecological changes of the world. Contemporary life throws up questions to which the church must respond, basing itself on the holy scriptures and the ecclesial Tradition. Among the problems the church must address is that of the interconnectedness of humanity with nature, especially at a time when general attention is focused on the catastrophic consequences of the exploitation of the world's resources and environmental pollution.

The patristic period produced incisive analyses of the conceptions of justice and peace in relation to God's divine act of creation. It stressed social commitment. Already in the sixth century St John Chrysostom vehemently condemned the apathy of Christians: "I see the body of the church stretched out on the ground like a corpse. I see its members, but like a lifeless body, none of them is functioning... We call each other sisters and brothers. We are members of the same body — in *name. In fact, however, we are divided like wild animals."*[6] Nothing else makes us imitators of Christ, only showing concern for the neighbour.[7] No miracle, no martyrdom can save us, if we do not have perfect agape (love) — solidarity with one another.[8]

"Be perfect as your heavenly Father is perfect." The patristic exposition of this maxim is consistent and explicit. Every effort towards personal *holiness* must have a social dimension. St John Chrysostom says that to seek only one's own salvation is the surest way of losing it. Vladimir Soloviev is only repeating him when he says: "Salvation is, for me, those who save others."

While the struggle continues, no single social form can ever be "dogmatized". Being the locus of the "Word which judges", the church stands above all existing political and economic regimes. It can live under religiously indifferent capitalism, as it does in many first-world societies; it can live the life of martyrdom under atheistic Marxism, as it did for many decades in a number of Central and Eastern European countries and in other parts of the world.

Christ's teaching

The New Testament does not extol any particular social system. Christ proclaims the coming of the kingdom, not any kingdom but his Father's, God's kingdom, and he has not a word to say about the political, social and economic institutions of his time. The difficult saying "render unto Caesar what is Caesar's and to God what is God's" (Matt. 22:21) at least teaches us not to confuse between the heavenly and earthly kingdoms. "Seek first the (heavenly) kingdom and all the rest (the earthly kingdom) will be added to you" (Matt. 6:33). This means that the *invisible* absolute validates the *visible* relative. But such relatives exist by relation to an absolute. Caesar is not Caesar except in relation to God. As St Paul says: "There is no authority except from God" (Rom. 13:1). In Dostoevsky's *The Possessed* someone tells an officer that God does not exist and he cries out: "If God does not exist, am I still a captain?"

Human beings receive their dignity from being a "theophany", and the love of humankind is justified because of what Nicolas Cabasilas, a Byzantine church writer, called God's "insane love" for humankind. By becoming flesh, God identifies himself with "man" and reveals that he has been created in God's image. But God is one and three, unity in plurality and diversity.

The reality of the people of God, become one in Christ, is the basis upon which the church formulates the *social dogma* of the koinonia/communion of all humanity, for it is in this communion that Christ is really present.

Without actually dealing with social structures, the gospel mediates a basic attitude for human relationships, the attitude which St John Chrysostom would later call sacramental. He says that the love of the neighbour, or better the "commitment to the neighbour", is a "sacrament" because under the visible form of the neighbour we receive the grace of the invisible presence of Christ. It is this presence which makes us everyone's neighbour. The whole last judgment passage concentrates on this "sacramental attitude" towards the sick, the hungry, the poor, the prisoners, etc.

But we are now in a completely new era. The problems of capitalism, technocracy, third-world hunger, war and religious conflicts have become burning issues for all churches. Eschatology can no longer mask laziness, theological obscurantism, indifference towards the world and passivity.

The threats we face represent the judgment of God on the world and the church. Every age has its own crisis and judgment, and this is what eschatology should study, not just the end of the world hidden in God's transcendent decree.

Eschatology, as it is developed in the holy scriptures and in the fathers' theology, demands solutions for our social problems and life concerns. The only efficacious solution for social and ethical problems is the one from the good news messages, for here God himself enjoins human beings to seize the kingdom and instal his eternal justice (cf. Isa. 55:3, 61:8). According to the church fathers, humankind is a *microcosm*, but the church, the Christian human community, is a *macro-anthropos*; it is the site of the *apokatastasis*, the sphere of the parousia and the "new world" in power and strength. Not just individual salvation, but the transfiguration of the human conscience is what the Christian message is all about.

This means that a new social order will not come out of human efforts, but rather from the Holy Spirit. A prayer invoking the Holy Spirit reads: "Heavenly King, Comforter, the Spirit of truth, who are present everywhere filling all things, Treasury of good things and Giver of life, *come* and dwell in us..." No theology or ecclesiology is possible, particularly with regard to the church and world, if one neglects to look at the world as a whole, created and supported by God. The church, whose essence is the divine-human fullness of life in the Holy Spirit, represents thus the macrocosms of the whole creation. Its unity in church reflects the unity of the "cosmos" created by God. In Christ and his body, the church of which he is the head, everything was created and reconciled (Col. 1:16-21).[9]

The "sacramental" dimension of the creation

"Thine own of thine own we offer unto thee." With these words the liturgy of St Chrysostom captures the heart of the Orthodox understanding of our relationship to creation and the Creator. Creation is of God. We do not own creation but are the free agents through whom creation is offered to the Creator.[10]

The purpose of creation is summed up in its worship of the Creator. This is most beautifully expressed in the Christmas hymns. "What shall we offer Thee, O Christ, who for our sake was seen on earth as man? For every thing, created by Thee, offers Thee thanks. The angels offer Thee their hymn; the heavens, the star, the Magi their gifts; the shepherds, their wonder; the earth, the cave; the wilderness, the manger, while we offer Thee a Virgin Mother; O pre-eternal God, have mercy upon us..."[11]

The whole of the universe worships and offers gifts to its Creator. In the very structure of the churches and the placing of the icons, mosaics or frescoes within them, we find a microcosm of the universe, which clarifies the role both of humanity and of the rest of creation in relation to God. For it is an expression not just of what is on earth today, but of what exists in heaven and what is to come — the eschatological promise and the redemptive transformation of all creation through the salvation wrought by Christ Jesus. This is expressed by St Paul in his letter to the Romans, chapter 8. As the Greek fathers have also taught, "God became man so that man can become God", and as St Gregory Palamas used to say "... creation can be transfigured by the action of the uncreated energies of God".

In worship the Orthodox church conveys this profound understanding of creation. In particular, the role of humanity as the "priesthood of creation" is most clearly shown.

The blessing of the waters shows us the sanctifying and redemptive power given to an element of creation through the invocation of the Holy Spirit by the church: "Therefore, O King, who lovest mankind, do Thou Thyself be present now as then through the descent of Thy Holy Spirit and sanctify this water. And confer upon it the grace of redemption, the blessing of the Jordan. Make it a source of incorruption, a gift of sanctification, a remission of sins, a protection against disease, a destruction to demons, inaccessible to the adverse powers and filled with angelic strength: that all who draw from it and partake of it may have it for the cleansing of their soul and body, for the healing of their passions, for the sanctification of their dwellings, and for every purpose that is expedient. For Thou art our God, who hast renewed through water and spirit our nature grown old through sin..."[12] Worship is about the celebration and use of all aspects of the senses. It is about sight, sound, taste, smell and touch. It uses and affirms the material — be that wood and paint, writing materials, bread and wine or burning incense.

"I shall not cease reverencing matter, by means of which my salvation has been achieved...,"[13] St John Damascus wrote in his essay defending icons. The use of materials to make icons and the presence of elements of the natural world in most icons — animals, plants, countryside, mountains, rivers — all affirm the God-given nature of creation, its transfiguration and its place with us in salvation. The anti-gnostic teachings of the church mean that the material world is held to be of God and is thus, in its essence, good.

The Byzantine churches were built in harmony with their natural surroundings. The art of architecture was not autonomous but, together with iconography and chant, contributed to the ethos of worship, giving it its physical, material expression. Thus it was that absolute symmetry was usually avoided; each architectural feature retained its own character while maintaining complete harmony with the overall conception.

At the centre of worship is the eucharist, the most sublime expression and experience of creation transformed by God's Spirit through redemption and worship. In the form of *bread* and *wine*, elements coming from creation moulded into new form by human hands are offered to God with the acknowledgment that all of creation is God's and that we are returning to God what is his. In the sense that this captures the primordial relationship of Adam to both God and creation, it is a sign of restoring that relationship of koinonia and, even more than that, a foretaste of the eschatological consummation of creation. When we partake of the body and blood of Christ, God meets us in the very substance of our relationship with creation and truly enters into the very being of our biological existence.[14]

From this we know that humanity occupies the most special place of all in creation — but is not the whole of creation. We know that as all is from God (cf. Job 38-39), we must respect creation and acknowledge that we are not its owners, but the ones who may enhance it by the wise use of our technology and skill only, however, so as to offer it again to its

Creator. There is no escape from the conclusion that we are responsible, before God, for the care of creation. It is our responsibility to protect its extraordinary richness and preserve, through wise use, its resources, not least those of energy, a crucial example of our power over creation and also of the potentially disastrous results of the greedy exercise of that power.

Meanwhile, just as the celebrant at the eucharist offers the fullness of creation and receives it back, as the blessing of grace in the form of the consecrated bread and wine, to share it with others, so we must be the channel through which God's grace is shared with all creation. The human being is simply, yet gloriously, the means for the expression of creation in its fullness and for mediating God's deliverance for all creation.

As the Syrian writer Saint Isaac taught, "the human man approaches ravening beasts and, when their gaze rests upon him, their wildness is tamed. They come up to him as to their Master, wag their heads and tails, and lick his hands and feet, for they smell coming from him that same scent that exhaled from Adam before the Fall, when they were gathered together before him and he gave them names in paradise. This was taken away from us, but Jesus has renewed it, and given it back to us through his coming. This it is that has sweetened the fragrance of the race of men."[15]

When we look today at our world, we see a completely different picture. Humanity's rebellion, pride and greed have shattered this primordial relationship. Humanity has ignored or discarded the church's understanding of our role as "priests of creation", for we behave like the robbers of creation. By doing so, we have destroyed not just species but entire eco-systems. Our world is facing a crisis of death and corruption to a degree never before experienced. The church fathers, while able to recognize the basic cause, *sin*, never had to experience such all-embracing and life-threatening consequences of sin as we do today.

"The earth is mourning, withering, the heavens are pining away with the earth," Isaiah declared. "The earth is defiled under its inhabitants' feet, for they have transgressed the law, violated the precept, broken the everlasting covenant. So a curse consumes the earth and its inhabitants suffer the penalty, that is why the inhabitants of the earth are burnt up and few are left" (Isa. 24:4-6).

Throughout the world, forests are being destroyed by fires and logging, wetlands are being drained for development and agriculture; species are disappearing as a result of greed and ignorance; natural resources are being wasted faster than they can be replenished; waters are being contaminated and skies polluted. This global crisis is threatening the very world upon which we human beings depend.

Humanity must return to a proper relationship with the Creator and his creation. This may well mean that just as a shepherd will, in times of greatest danger, lay down his life for his flock, so human beings may need to forego part of their wants and needs in order that the survival of the natural world can be assured. This is a new situation and a new challenge. It calls for humanity to bear some of the pain of creation as well as to enjoy and celebrate it. It calls first and foremost for *repentance* — but of an order not previously understood by many.

"Love all God's creation," wrote Fyodor Dostoevsky, "the whole of it and every grain of sand. Love every leaf, every ray of God's light! Love the animals, love the plants, love everything. If you love everything, you will perceive the divine mystery in things. And once you have perceived it, you will begin to comprehend it ceaselessly, more, more and more every day. And you will come at last to love the whole world with an abiding universal love. Love the whole world with an abiding universal love. Love the animals: God has given them the rudiments of thought and untroubled joy. Do not, therefore, trouble it, do not torture them, do not deprive them of their joy, do not go against God's intent."

But repentance without action is meaningless. As Christ says: "Many will call me, 'Lord, Lord'" (cf. Rom. 10:12), but only those "who do the will of my Father shall enter heaven" (cf. Acts 2:21; Joel 2:32). So we must have recourse to an ascetic approach to give expression to this repentance.

The monastic and ascetic traditions of Orthodoxy offer important insights here. They develop sensitivity to the suffering of all creation. There are many stories of saints living side by side with other creatures, sharing their everyday life. They offer a celebratory use of the resources of creation in a spirit of *enkratia* (self-control, voluntary abstention). Within such a tradition many have experienced a more profound joy and a more lasting satisfaction than the ephemeral pleasures of a consumer society. The emphasis in the cenobitic, monastic tradition on community rather than individual life is central to a balanced understanding of our daily needs.

It is in this asceticism that many people will experience the pain which is that of the shepherd willing to suffer for the sake of his flock. For without substantial changes in our life-style and our expectations, we cannot fulfill our God-given role in creation.

Thus, Orthodox spirituality underlines the notion of solidarity with the world and is always eminently realistic. It has nothing to do with the attitudes of rigid conservatism and other-worldliness which deny the reality of the world and encourage contemplation through a form of monasticism that is wholly inward-looking and unrelated to the world. Monasticism and the contemplative life are, for the Orthodox, simply signs of the end of history and of the eschatological dimension of the church inaugurated in time by the arrival of the Paraclete. It is a vivifying liturgical presence of continuous prayer and doxology that humanity addresses to the work of Christ while awaiting his second coming in glory.

Humanity's failure

Justice and peace are a prerequisite for freedom. But what is freedom? The word is normally used to indicate the capacity to choose from two or more possibilities. Why choose between what is given to me and not be free to create my own possibilities? We can see how the question of freedom and that of creation out of nothing are inter-related; if one creates out of something, one is presented by something given; if one creates out of nothing, one is free in the absolute sense of the term.

But what about the human being? "Man" (anthropos) is by definition a creature. This means that he is presented with a given reality. The fact that in the biblical account of creation they emerge at the end of the creative process makes human beings doubly restricted; the world is given to them, and God the Creator is given to them, too. They can choose what they like, but they cannot avoid the fact of givenness. Are they therefore free in an absolute sense?

It is at this point that the idea of the *imago Dei* emerges. Christian anthropology, since its earliest days, insisted that "man" was created "in the image and likeness of God". The idea, or rather the expression, appears for the first time in the Genesis account of creation. It was taken up by the church fathers, and Christian theology has expounded it throughout history. Various meanings have been given, among them the one that identifies the image of God in man with his reason. It is clear that if we speak of an image of and link to God, we must refer inevitably to something which characterizes God in an exclusive way. If the *imago Dei* consists in something to be found outside God, it is not an image of God. We are therefore talking about a quality pertaining to God and not to creation.

This forces us to seek the *imago Dei* in freedom. If freedom is taken in the way in which it is applied to God — which is what we should do if we are talking about an image of God — then, we are talking about absolute freedom in the sense of not being confronted with anything given. But this would be absurd. For man is a creature and what he is and has is given.

It is at this point that another category, pertaining exclusively to the definition of the human, emerges. It is tragedy, the tragic. Tragedy is the impasse created by freedom reaching out to a fulfilment which it is unable to reach. The tragic applies only to the human condition and is not applicable to God or to the rest of creation. It is impossible to have a complete definition of man without reference to the tragic, and this is related directly to the subject of freedom. Dostoevsky, that great Christian prophet of modern times, put his finger on this crucial issue when he placed the following words in the mouth of Kirilov, one of the heroes in *The Possessed*: "Everyone who wants to attain complete freedom must be daring enough to kill himself... This is the final limit of freedom; that is all, there is nothing beyond it. Who dares to kill himself becomes God. Everyone can do this and thus cause God to cease to exist, and then nothing will exist at all."

If man wishes to be God, he has to cope with the givenness of his own being. As long as he is faced with the fact that he is "created", which means that his being is given to him, he cannot be said to be free in the absolute sense.

Yet man in so many ways desires to attain such an absolute freedom; it is in fact precisely this that distinguishes him from the animal world. Why did God give him such an unfulfillable drive? In fact, many people would wish, for themselves as well as for others, that they were not free in this absolute sense. The Christian church itself has produced throughout the centuries devices by which man, particularly the Christian, would be so domesticated that he would give up all claims to absolute freedom, leaving such claims only to God. But certainly, if God gave such a drive to man, if he made him in his own image, he must have had a purpose. We suggest that this purpose has to do precisely with the survival of creation, with man's call to be "the priest of creation", as we said earlier.

Christian anthropology speaks of the first man, Adam, placed in paradise with the mandate to exercise dominion over creation. That he was to do this in and through his *freedom* is implied by the fact that he was presented with a decision to obey or disobey a certain commandment by God. This commandment involved the invitation to exercise the freedom implied in the *imago Dei*, i.e. to act as if man were God. This Adam did, and the result was the fall and sin.

But why did man fall by exercising what God himself had given him, namely freedom? Would it have been better for him and for creation had he not exercised, but rather sacrificed this absolute kind of freedom? Would it not perhaps have been better for all of us if Adam had been content with a relative freedom as befits a creature? Did the tragedy of the Fall consist in the *excess* of human freedom?

The answer commonly given to these questions is a positive one: yes, Adam exceeded the limits of his freedom, and that was why he fell. It is for this reason that Adam's Fall is commonly associated with Adam's fault, a fault to be understood forensically.

There are various ways of interpreting the Fall other than the one involving a blame on Adam for having exceeded the limits of his freedom. We shall perhaps have to abandon forensic categories of guilt. It may be more logical, more consistent with our view of the *imago Dei*, if we followed not St Augustine but rather St Irenaeus in this respect.

St Irenaeus took a very "philanthrophic", a very compassionate, view of Adam's Fall. He thought of him as a child placed in paradise in order to grow to adulthood by exercising his freedom. But he was deceived, and he did the wrong thing. What does this mean? It was not a question of exceeding the limits of freedom, but rather of applying absolute freedom in the wrong way. That is very different from saying that Adam ought to have adjusted the exercise of his freedom to his creaturely limitations. For had he adjusted his freedom this way, he would have lost the drive to absolute freedom, whereas now he can still have it, but readjusts and reorients it.

The implications are far-reaching and include a number of consequences for the legalistic views of sin which, not by accident, go hand in hand with cries for relativized freedom. Man was given the drive to absolute freedom, the *imago Dei*, not for himself but for creation itself.

Thus, the whole cosmos is ready to receive the "new creation" which is celebrating God's manifestation on the earth and opens new horizons for revolution. It is ready to receive this "new creation" only with justice and peace and unity of humankind. Humanity becomes a receiver of the "new heaven and the new earth" which tries to be transformed into a new reality and to overcome *death* and *sin*. The whole world is expecting this new transformation, transfiguration, the day of the "new Epiphany".

A "personal" approach to creation

We have noted that creation does not possess any natural means of survival. This means that if left to itself, it will die. The only way to avoid this would be the restoration of the koinonia/communion with the eternal God. This, however, would require a movement of transcendence beyond the boundaries of creation. It would require, in other words, *justice, freedom and peace* in the absolute sense. If creation were to attempt its survival only through obedience to God, in the sense of its realizing, so to say, its own limitations and not attempting to transcend them, as John Zizioulas would say,[16] its survival would require the miracle of a *Deus ex machina* intervention. If we accept the view that the world needs to transcend itself in order to survive (which is the logical consequence of having accepted that the world had a beginning), we need to find a way of achieving this transcendence. This is what the *imago Dei* was given for.

The transcendence of the limits of creation as the condition for its survival requires on the part of creation a drive to absolute freedom. The fact that this drive was given to man made the whole creation rejoice, in the words of St Paul "awaiting with eager expectation the revelation of the glory of the children of God", i.e. of man. Because man, unlike the angels (who are also regarded as endowed with freedom), forms an organic part of the material world, being the highest point in its evolution, and he is able to carry with him the whole creation to its transcendence. The fact that the human being is also an animal, as Darwin has reminded us, far from being an insult, constitutes — in spite, perhaps, of Darwin's intentions — the *sine qua non* condition for his glorious *mission in creation*. If man gave up his claim to absolute freedom, the whole creation would automatically lose its hope for survival.

But how can man liberate creation from its boundaries and lead it to survival through his freedom? At this point Christian theology has to rely on its doctrinal resources rather heavily to avoid as far as possible making it a matter of "esoteric" language understood only by those who have access to it by virtue of their doctrinal commitment.[17]

Reference has already been made to man's tendency to create a new world. This tendency continues his specific characteristic compared with animals and is, in this sense, an essential expression of the image of God in him. This means that man wishes to pass through his own hands everything that exists and make it his own. Making it "his own" may mean that man can use creation for his own benefit, in which case, by being placed in man's hand creation is not truly lifted to the level of the human, but subjected to it. This is one of the ways in which man can understand God's commandment to have dominion over the earth: it could be called the *utilitarian* way.

Anthropologically speaking, man could cut himself off from nature as if he did not belong to it himself. The utilitarian attitude to creation would then go hand in hand with the view that man differs from the rest of creation through his capacity to dissociate himself from it rather than to associate himself with it. It could also go together with the possibility of denying God and divinizing man. Atheism and man's dissociation from nature would thus be shown to be interconnected. They both spring from the *imago Dei* and confirm the view that the difference between man and creation relates to the question of freedom. Needless to say, the ecological problem is rooted deeply in this kind of anthropology. An understanding of the world as man's *possession* — a means of drawing from it self-satisfaction and pleasure — is what taking the world in man's hands means in this case.

Science and technology then signify the employment of man's intellectual superiority for the purpose of discovering ways and means by which he may draw the biggest possible profit from creation for his own purposes. In this case, a theology based on the assumption that the essence of man lies in his intellect would be responsible, with science and technology, for the ecological problem.

Making the world pass through the hands of man may mean something entirely different from what humanity and the world ask for. Of course, man would still use creation as a source from which he would draw the basic elements necessary for his life — such as food, clothing, building of houses, etc. But to all this he would give a dimension which is "personal". [18]

Man (anthropos) cannot be understood in isolation but only in relation to something or someone else. A *personal* approach to creation as distinct from an *individualistic* one would regard the human being as someone whose particular identity arises from his relation with what is not human. This could be both or either God and/or creation. It is not, therefore, in juxtaposition to nature but in association with it that man would find his specific identity. Man would be other than nature, not by separating himself from it, but by relating himself to it. This will become immediately evident in culture; the way man eats or dresses or builds his house and will involve a close relationship with what is not human, with what is significantly called "the environment". A personal approach to creation would thus elevate the material world to the level of man's existence. The material creation would in this way be liberated from its own limitations and, by being placed in the hands of man, it would itself acquire a personal dimension; it would be *humanized*.

The personal dimension, as distinct from the individual one, involves what we may call *hypostasization* and *catholicity*. These terms are technical in theology but they can be easily translated into non-theological language. A *hypostasis* is an identity which embodies and expresses in itself the totality of nature. The personal approach makes every being unique and irreplaceable, whereas the individual approach makes of it a number in statistics. If man acts as a person, rather than as an individual, in dealing with creation, he not only lifts it up to the level of the human, but he sees it as a totality, as a catholicity of inter-related entities. Creation is, thus, able to realize the unity which, as natural science observes today, is inherent in its very structure.

Therefore, the personhood in man demands constantly that creation be treated as something destined by God not only to survive but also to be "fulfilled" in and through man's hands. There are two basic dimensions in personhood, both of which enable the human being to fulfill his role as the link between God and creation. One is what may be called its *hypostatic* aspect, through which the world is integrated and embodied into a unified reality. The other is what may be called its *ecstatic* aspect by virtue of which the world, by being referred to God and offered to him as "his own", reaches itself to infinite possibilities. This constitutes the basis of what can be called *man's priesthood*. By taking the world into his hands and creatively integrating it and by referring it to God, man liberates creation from its limitations and lets it truly be. Thus, in being the priest of creation, man is also a creator and, perhaps, it may be said that in all of his truly creative activities there is hidden a para-priestly character. In speaking of "priesthood", therefore, we speak of a broader existential attitude encompassing all human activities that involve a conscious or even unconscious manifestation of these two aspects of personhood: the *hypo-static* and the *ec-static*, in the sense we have just described them.

To put all this in terms of Christian doctrine, Christians believe that what Adam failed to do Christ did. Christ is regarded as the embodiment of the *recapitulation (anakephalaiosis)* of all creation and, therefore, as the *man par excellence* and the saviour of the world. We regard him, because of this, as the true "image of God" and we associate him with the final fate of the world. We, therefore, believe that in the person of Christ we see the priest of creation, the model of man's proper relation to the natural world.

On the basis of this belief, a community is formed which takes from creation certain elements (the bread and the wine) which are offered to God with the solemn declaration "Thine own of thine own we offer unto Thee", thus recognizing that creation does not belong to us but to God, who is its only "owner". By so doing, we believe that creation is brought back into relation with God the Creator.

Man's priesthood

It would appear that the ecological crisis is a crisis of culture. It is a crisis that has to do with the loss of the sacredness of nature in our culture. I can see only two ways of overcoming this. One would be the way of paganism. The pagan regards the world as sacred because it is permeated by divine presence; he therefore respects it (to the point of worshipping it explicitly or implicitly) and does not want to do damage to it. But he never worries about its fate either: he believes in its eternity. He is also unaware of any need for the transformation of nature. The world is good as it stands and possesses all that is necessary for its survival.

The other way is what we have tried to describe here as the Christian way. The Christian regards the world as sacred because it stands in dialectical relationship with God: thus he respects it (without worshipping it), and regards the human being as the only possible link between God and creation, a link that can either bring nature to communion with God and thus sanctify it, or turn it ultimately towards man — or nature itself — and condemn it to the state of a thing whose meaning and purpose are exhausted with giving satisfaction to human beings.

Of these two ways, the second one enjoins on man a heavy responsibility for the fate of creation. The first one sees man as part of the world; the second, by considering man to be the crucial link between the world and God, sees him as the only person in creation, i.e. as the only one who would be so deeply respectful of the impersonal world as not simply to "preserve" it, but to cultivate it and embody it in forms of culture which will elevate it to eternal survival. Unless we decide to return to paganism, this seems to be the only way to respect once again the sacredness of nature and face the ecological crisis. For it is now clear that the model of human domination over nature, as we have it in our present-day technological ethos, will not ensure the survival of God's creation.

The apostolic community of Jerusalem up to the year 70 succeeded in practising, as Paul Evdokimov used to say, a voluntary "communion of love"[19] which remains a model and source of inspiration. Furthermore, in spite of the fact that the expectation of the parousia minimized the need for material care, the apostles chose women and men for the social ministry, the *diakonia*, of the church — a charismatic service quite distinct from the *priestly office* and one which would later become the task of the parish laity.

Later on, the Renaissance brought religious and economic individual-ism. Spirituality now took no interest in the problems of work, in the body or the material and increasingly secularized world. The capitalist system encountered no moral resistance from the already decadent Christian society which tolerated, and then sanctioned, economic and industrial exploitation.

With the French Revolution the social ideal temporarily took a hostile attitude to all religious, mainly European, influence. Socialism inherited this attitude even though it had its origins in medieval evangelical poverty movements. St Simon and other utopians were Christian romantics, and the climate was unconsciously religious. When Marx transformed social-ism into historical and dialectical materialism, the conscience of the Western church was finally awakened: Leo XIII spoke of an "economic immorality"; Pius XI condemned certain principles of capitalism; Paul VI followed the doctrine of his predecessors, but put a much stronger emphasis on the opposition between human community and economic individualism. And John Paul II, with the Centesimus Annus encyclical on Rerum Novarum, renewed the interest of the Roman Catholic Church for a new evangelization of Europe based upon new economic systems, in view of the changes in Central and Eastern Europe, and unmasked the persistant interest of his church in "a new conquest" — as many Orthodox theologians strongly used to believe — in a new fertile era with new possibilities.

Today, why not earlier?

Since the end of the sixteenth century, and especially after the painful Soviet experience, the mystical belief in the "utopia of an earthly paradise" has given way to disillusionment and deep discouragement. Only Christian personalism has a chance of giving an adequate answer and resolving the present problems, for, unlike capitalism, individualism and Marxist collectivism, it has insisted for many decades on the basic worth of the human person as subject (not object) and sought his fulfilment only in communion with all other individuals. Here is the so-called *sobornost* that Orthodox theology used to affirm.

Looking at the future: an ocean of signs of hope

The Orthodox church has rejected the way of papal encyclicals and Anglo-Saxon social activism. Having rediscovered its image as a poor, servant church, it purged itself of every "triumphant and terrorist" notion of "religion". This was its only adequate expression of its mystery: to follow in the footsteps of the Christ "oikonomos", the sorrowful and suffering servant of Yahweh. Perhaps there is, even now, no more disarming answer to modern forms of atheism.

The tragedy for the church was that it accepted social reforms only after the Bolshevik revolution. The Swiss socialist Ragaz wrote on the tragic split between those who believed in God but were not interested in his kingdom and the atheists who wanted to build the kingdom but did not believe in God.

But we are today entering a completely new epoch, an epoch in which we have much to do.

According to St John's gospel, Jesus at the last supper not only promised that he would remain with his disciples, but also that he would send them the Paraclete, the Spirit, as encourager, supporter, consoler and giver of life.

The Spirit promised by Jesus shapes the eucharistic Christian and the eucharistic church from top to bottom. It arouses thankful remembrance; it arouses readiness, watchfulness and discernment for the present time of salvation; it gives us the strength to become, in keeping with these promises, witnesses and instruments of the continual coming of God's kingdom.

Therefore, in God's Spirit, we are a "new creation", capable of bringing forth the fruits of the Spirit: love, joy, peace, patience, kindness, goodness, faithfulness, gentleness, self-control (Gal. 5:22).

The Spirit's fruits are our common heritage; they are capable of challenging Christians and churches to respond to the needs of today's world, to preserve the integrity of the creation, to take care of the environment, to struggle against all threats to true peace and justice for the sake of the whole humanity.

NOTES

[1] Cf. the statement of the Eastern and Oriental Orthodox representatives and participants in the Seoul convocation (1990) which strongly expressed their concerns on the issues of "covenant", "covenanting" and "renewing our covenant with God".

[2] Cf. "Creation and the Kingdom of God" (consultation with Faith and Order), Church and Society Document no. 89, eds D. Gosling & G. Limouris, Geneva, WCC, 1988.

[3] Cf. Martien E. Brinkmann, "Creation and Sacrament", in *Exchange*, vol. 19/3, December 1990, p.205.

[4] G. Limouris ed., *Justice, Peace and the Integrity of Creation: Insights from Orthodoxy*, Geneva, WCC, 1990. This volume includes reports and papers presented at two inter-Orthodox consultations in preparation for the Seoul convocation (Sofia, 1987 and Minsk, 1989).

[5] Cf. message of the Ecumenical Patriarch Dimitrios I, "On the Day of the Protection of the Environment", Phanar, 1989: "In view of this (world) situation, the church of Christ cannot remain unmoved... we paternally urge... all the faithful in the world to admonish themselves and their children to respect and protect the natural environment, and all who are entrusted with the responsibility of governing the nations to act without delay, taking all necessary measures for the protection and preservation of natural creation." See text in English in *Orthodoxy and the Ecological Crisis*, Gland, Switzerland, WWF International, 1990, pp.3-4.

[6] Homily on 2 Cor. 27, ch. 4.

[7] Homily on 1 Cor. 25, ch. 3.

[8] *Ibid.*, ch. 4.

[9] Cf. G. Limouris, "The Integrity of Creation in a World of Change Today: Patristic Perspectives", in *Theologia*, vol. 61/1-2, 1990, pp.19ff.

[10] Cf. *Orthodoxy and the Ecological Crisis, op. cit.*, pp.4-13.

[11] Hymn of Christmas vespers.

[12] Prayer for the blessing of waters at Epiphany.

[13] *On the Images*, I, 16.

[14] Cf. John Zizioulas, "The Eucharistic Understanding of the World and the Modern Man", in *Christian Symposium*, 1967, pp.183ff (in Greek).

[15] *Ascetical Homilies*, Homily 77.

[16] Cf. Metropolitan John of Pergamon (Zizioulas), "Preserving God's Creation", three lectures on theology and ecology given at King's College, London, UK, January 1989 (mimeographed). We are grateful to the author for the use of substantial material in this paper.

[17] *Ibid.*

[18] Cf. Zizioulas, *op. cit.*

[19] Cf. P. Evdokimov, "The Social Dimension of Orthodox Ecclesiology", in *Theology Digest*, vol. XVIII, no. 1, spring 1970, p.45.

From Seoul to Santiago

The Unity of the Church and JPIC

Thomas F. Best

Faith and Order Commissioner Bishop T.S.A. Annobil of Ghana was once asked why *Baptism, Eucharist and Ministry*[1] — with its focus on church doctrine and practice — was important for "everyday Christians" in his country. In reply he told the following story:

> An illiterate old woman reflecting on the eucharist confronted me with a serious theological argument and asked some serious questions. She told me that since the priest of her own denomination could visit their congregation only once a month, she sometimes went to the service at another church since their priest (who had a car) was able to visit there more often.
>
> She said: "On one such occasion Father X visited and that morning I felt spiritually hungry so I went to the other service. When it was time for holy communion I felt I should partake, so I got up to go to the altar. The priest, who knew me personally and also knew that I am from another church, sent one of the servers to tell me not to go for communion.
>
> "I was not only embarrassed but I felt spiritually rejected and let down. What worries me is that when there was a shortage of food in 1984, Father X brought rice and beans to this village and when I went to the mission house, he gave me enough rice and beans to last me and my family for about two weeks. And yet when I got up to go for communion he refused me.
>
> "Bishop, I do not believe that you bishops, priests and ministers make the things of the altar holy, they are made holy by God. Is the Jesus you clergymen preach the same Jesus who went about doing good, the Jesus who received the Samaritan woman, Mary Magdalene, the publican Zacchaeus, the

Jesus who was a friend of publicans and sinners? I do not believe that the Lord himself would have refused me."

The old lady concluded by saying, "May God's kingdom come quickly and then we will know who is right."[2]

This extraordinary account links vividly the churches' search for visible unity with their common calling to prophetic witness and service. It shows that unity is the only lasting basis for common Christian witness and service; that work towards unity is incomplete unless it issues in common witness and service; and that the people of God, however much they value and benefit from common Christian witness and service, will yearn for and finally demand a greater degree of visible unity. How striking that this testimony comes not from professors of theology and ecclesiology, but from the instinctive Christian wisdom of an "unlettered", "ordinary" church member! The grassroots have spoken.

The two world Christian gatherings mentioned in the title of this essay — the Seoul world convocation on "Justice, Peace and the Integrity of Creation" held in 1990 and the fifth world conference on Faith and Order, to be held in Santiago de Compostela, Spain, in August 1993 — are focusing widespread attention on the relation between the search for visible church unity and the churches' work for justice, peace and for the preservation of creation. This is the latest stage of a discussion, which is as old as the ecumenical movement itself, on the relation between the unity of the church and the churches' witness and service in the world. It is important to begin from the common ecumenical conviction that the two aspects are both integral to the nature of the church and essential to the ecumenical task today.

The imperative to unity, witness and service

Although the form and shape of Christian unity is intensely debated today, the imperative for unity is not at issue. The search for Christian unity is not an "addition" to the Christian faith, but an essential part of it, an integral element of the churches' life. It is necessary on at least six grounds: (1) *Biblically*, in obedience to Christ's desire and command that his disciples might "be one... in order that the world may believe" (John 17:20-24), and the New Testament picture of the church struggling to "be of one heart and mind..." (Acts 4:32), and truly the body of Christ; (2) *theologically*, recognizing that the life of the church is grounded in the vision of the life of the Trinity, a life of unity-in-diversity and sharing, a vision belied by the divisions among Christians; (3) *ecclesiologically*, in recognition that the harmful divisions between churches are wounds in the body of Christ, crying out for healing, a healing which involves just behaviour and right relationships between the different members of the body; (4) *doxologically*, in obedience to God and to the praise and glory of God, who wills that God's people be one; (5) for the sake of *mission*, because disunity contradicts the Christian proclamation of wholeness and healing based on the restoration of right relationships among human beings and between humanity and the rest of the created order, and may degenerate into competition among rival Christian groups;[3] and (6) *to enable a more effective witness*, because disunity leads to duplication of effort, if not unseemly competition, while co-operation and united effort enables Christians to speak as one, whether to persons seeking earnestly the meaning of life or to the "principalities and powers" governing an indifferent or hostile society.

Note that organizational or bureaucratic needs are not included on this list; indeed church union efforts based primarily on the hope that they will lead to a more "efficient" or "streamlined" institution are unlikely to prosper in the long run. Nor are financial motivations finally helpful. Church unions are sometimes promoted as a way to save administrative and building costs: they do not.

The search for unity arises, ultimately, from the conviction that our institutional divisions are a scandal, a contradiction of the very message we proclaim. In this search we are rejecting not the necessary variety which enriches the one body of Christ, but the harmful divisions which are wounds in and of that body. We are rejecting the fact that so many Christians in the world today are unable to share the eucharist — the supper of their common Lord — with one another; the theological claim of the WCC Vancouver assembly that "Christ — the life of the world — unites heaven and earth, God and world, spiritual and secular"[4] "renders even more scandalous the fact that Christians are not able to come together at the Lord's table".[5] We are rejecting the fact that, between many churches even today, membership and ministry are not mutually recognized. We are rejecting a too-narrow and limited self-understanding of the churches, which tempts them to identify Christian truth too uniquely with a particular theological, cultural or ethnic situation and makes them prey to being used by one side or another in secular, ethnic or cultural conflicts.

And many of those most deeply committed to the search for unity are driven by some special personal experience, an experience of sharing a common identity beyond or in spite of the Christian divisions, something which has disturbed the comfortable accommodation which we have made to those divisions, and which has offered them a glimpse and foretaste of Christian communion beyond institutional and confessional boundaries. Consider, for example, this testimony from Malaysia:

> Ecumenism there was born in the common experience of Christian leaders interned in Changi prison during the second world war. [Up to then] their denominational differences had centred on varying interpretations of baptism, communion, etc. When there was no bread, no cup, no wine to be had, when the only water for baptism was that from the toilet in their cell, they experienced their primal unity as Christians rather than their separate identities as Anglicans or Methodists. [6]

Those who share this "divine discontent with disunity" experience our continuing separation as painful and wrong; they will hunger for unity, and not grow weary in working for it.

But the Christian imperative to witness and service is equally fundamental to the identity and life of the churches today. Although convictions may differ as to the specific goals to be achieved, and the particular methods to achieve them, no church within the broad ecumenical family would now deny that it is called to witness and struggle for justice between individuals and groups, for a true peace (a shalom rooted in justice), and for the protection and nurturing of creation. Because God wills that God's creatures live in harmony and right relationships with one another, and that God's creation should flourish and prosper, Christians are called to translate these convictions into practical results in specific situations here and now. Thus the call to witness and service is not something "extra" to the Christian faith, but an essential expression of that faith and integral to the life of the church.

The conviction that the call to unity and the call to witness and service are inseparably interlinked has, of course, been central to the ecumenical movement from its beginnings. This was affirmed already at the first world conference on Faith and Order in Lausanne in 1927. This saw the early stages of a discussion which was to lead, in 1948, to the formation of the World Council of Churches. Some at Lausanne felt that a council incorporating these two dimensions of the ecumenical movement should be formed quickly while, as the report noted, "others believe that, for the present, it would be wiser for the movements represented by Stockholm [Life and Work, e.g. common witness and service] and Lausanne [Faith and Order, e.g. the search for visible unity] to develop in independence, each following its own way; *but there is general agreement that ultimately life, work, faith and order are expressions of an existing spiritual unity, and that each requires the other for its complete fruition".*[7]

But although it has been widely recognized that the linking of unity, justice and service is both required by our faith and essential to the health and wholeness of the ecumenical movement, there has been a persistent tendency to focus on one or another side of the ecumenical coin. These two emphases, embodied in movements in the early years of this century, have become institutionalized in the lives of the churches and ecumenical organizations today. Indeed they often co-exist as different "divisions" within a particular church, church council or Christian organization, each having its separate structures of supervision and funding, and often feeling a sense of rivalry if not competition with those who carry the "other part" of the ecumenical agenda.

This continuing division has been rejected again and again by the Faith and Order movement, most recently in *Church and World*, the culminating text from the first phase of the study programme on "The Unity of the Church and the Renewal of Human Community" (1984):

> These two issues — the search for unity and the search for renewal — are often seen as being separate and distinct, and with this goes the tendency to consider either one *or* the other as the most important or urgent ecumenical task. This contradicts, however, the long-held ecumenical conviction that God's will, revealed in Jesus Christ, calls the churches both to visible unity among themselves and to common witness and service for the renewal of human community.[8]

It is widely felt that the ecumenical movement stands today at the crossroads, facing difficult choices and needing a surge of fresh inspiration and energy. There are many reasons for this widespread sense of ecumenical malaise, but the continuing division between the ecumenical forces committed to unity and those focused on witness and service is surely part of the problem. Thus we must urgently seek ways to bring these two dimensions into creative dialogue, and learn to see them as part of one ecumenical movement.

Seoul and the JPIC process: its ecumenical significance

Despite its practical and conceptual difficulties — these have been discussed only too thoroughly and need not be repeated here — the JPIC process has been of great significance to the churches and to the ecumenical movement. Creative theological and ethical reflection, and important awareness-building, came through the preparatory meetings in Latin America, the Pacific, and particularly Europe; from Reformed,

Orthodox and Roman Catholic confessional perspectives; and from women's regional meetings.[9] The commitments made at the Seoul world convocation on JPIC[10] have great symbolic power, as well as considerable tactical and political potential for bringing Christian pressure to bear on crucial ethical issues today. But even more instructive, I believe, than the specific results from Seoul are three ways in which the JPIC process sought to bring fresh life and energy to the ecumenical scene.

First, it sought to restore a sense of the ecumenical endeavour as a *movement*, as the people of God moving together, rather than a bureaucratic system "belonging" (in a negative, restricted sense) only to the institutional church. Consider this stirring call from the world convocation on JPIC in Seoul:

> Now is the time to recognize that there is a long process still before us. We will take to our churches and our movements the affirmations and commitments we have made in Seoul, inviting others to join us. Together with them we struggle for the realization of our vision. We are accountable to one another and to God. We pray that we do not miss the *kairos* to which we have been led by God.[11]

These are "marching orders". They include an implicit criticism of the institutionalization of ecumenical work, a call for the deeper involvement of the whole church in the process, and a plea for a renewed sense of excitement and commitment. It should be noted that this was not just a reaction against the classic "unity movement", but was directed also against the ecumenical aid and development structures — which can be every bit as bureaucratized and institutionalized as the organizations of the "theologians" and "professors" who seem, to some, mainly interested in the number of doctrines which can fit on the head of a pin.

Second, Seoul expressed a powerful longing for renewed connections, for fresh linkages with others working for the same cause. As its final document noted, "not every church or group can be engaged at all points of the struggle for JPIC at the same time. Each engages at some one point knowing that by so doing it belongs to a covenant solidarity that is worldwide."[12] Thus against the present widespread sense of apathy and despair, a fear that the problems faced by the world and the churches are simply too big for anyone to tackle, Seoul insisted that Christians and others of good will could make a difference. In "covenant solidarity" lay hope and new energy for the struggle.

Third, the JPIC process offered those working in three crucial but disparate areas of human need a sense of wholeness and integration.

Indeed it broke down barriers within the ethical/social "wing" of the ecumenical movement. As is well known, there had been inevitable tensions between those struggling with justice issues and those working for peace (particularly in the context of the super-power confrontations of the Cold War); stereotypically these issues were focused in the Southern and Northern hemispheres respectively. Thus the Seoul message sought to be genuinely creative, to proclaim a breakthrough, in saying that "there are no competitive efforts for justice, peace and the integrity of creation. There is one single global struggle."[13] Much of the power of the JPIC vision came from its uniting of related, but differently organized and sometimes competing agendas.

JPIC: the limits of a common vision

Thus the JPIC process has important lessons to teach the whole ecumenical movement. And yet it also revealed some limits to common ecumenical witness and service. This was apparent especially with the two theological concepts which should have provided the foundation of the entire JPIC process: the ideas of covenant and of JPIC as a "conciliar process". It is also important to see what we can learn from the problems of JPIC.

The Seoul convocation had to admit that "in spite of all the attempts made, there were still some unresolved differences in the understanding of 'covenant'".[14] The use of this term was grounded in the experience of delegates to the WCC sixth assembly in Vancouver in 1983, where Christians from various regions of the world made solemn commitments to one another ("covenanted" together) to work for specific religious/ethical and political goals. The term comes especially from Reformed theology with its creative focus on the biblical theme of God's covenant with God's people. But as the JPIC process developed it proved difficult for some confessional families. For several it was not familiar or current theological coinage; and some of those comfortable theologically with the image of God's covenant with Israel — a covenant between a superior and a dependent party — could not see how it applied to covenants made between human beings or between churches, that is, between equal parties. Indeed to some the biblical image inevitably implied a relationship between a "superior" and an "inferior", and this was exactly the impression which those covenanting between North and South, developed and developing countries, "rich" and "poor", were trying to avoid.

Another problem came in applying and extending the Vancouver model of covenanting. This had been based primarily upon personal commitments made between individuals to achieve specific goals on which they already basically agreed. It proved difficult to translate this personal dynamic into the lives of churches or Christian organizations, which are large and complex institutions, encompassing a bewildering variety of views and requiring maddeningly slow deliberative processes to arrive at a collective position. The JPIC process simply did not have enough time to deal with these realities of institutional life. True, "it was indeed remarkable that this diverse group [at the Seoul convocation] was able to enter into and set in motion a global process of covenanting as an expression of their mutual commitment...";[15] and that is to be celebrated. Yet the process fell seriously short of the level of engagement of the churches *as churches* which had been hoped for.

Perhaps even more serious was the fact that, as the Seoul final document puts it, "the term 'conciliar process'... had to be abandoned for theological reasons".[16] The use of this highly-charged theological term had pointed to the earnest desire to make JPIC not merely a personal but also an official process, a vehicle through which the churches could grow together, formally and officially, in their common commitment to the struggle against injustice, violence and the manifold threats to life. Some saw a parallel to the Faith and Order study process on "Baptism, Eucharist and Ministry", through which many WCC member churches explored the degree of ecumenical convergence in these areas of church doctrine and practise:[17] could not the churches grow together also in the field of social witness? There was indeed a growing consensus in some areas — that theological support for apartheid was, in quite a precise sense, heretical; that there is a Christian responsibility to respect and to protect creation. Could not the agreement among the churches in these social and ethical areas be deepened and formalized through a process of ecumenical discussion? Could not the process lead beyond discussion to common commitment and even action?

Again the time factor was a significant problem. There was not sufficient time to consolidate and extend the consensus emerging in some specific areas amongst the churches. It should be remembered that BEM was almost 15 years old (in fact a first draft had already been through one round of response) when it was sent officially to the churches in 1981. Indeed the process of translating the text into local languages, not to mention receiving responses and evaluating them, continues even today.

But more serious than this were the difficulties inherent in the term "conciliar" itself. It is an exceedingly sensitive term, with many meanings and very dear to the theological hearts of the churches. WCC central committee moderator Archbishop Aram Keshishian discerns no fewer than five meanings in current ecumenical usage.[18] The two fundamental senses of the term were already well expressed by the Faith and Order Commission meeting at Bristol in 1967:

> The conciliar process in the ancient church took place in a still unbroken fellowship, generally speaking... [there were differences, but] the conciliar process in the ancient church took place, nevertheless, on the basis of the existing fellowship. Today, however, the point of departure is one of plural ecclesiastical communities in confrontation with one another. They differ in their confession of the truth... The restoration of fellowship is the task with which they see themselves faced in the ecumenical movement.[19]

That is, for some the term "council" refers to the "fellowship of divided churches", gathered in modern-day "councils of churches" for common reflection, witness and service. These bodies, at the local, national, regional and world level, provide an essential forum for churches to co-operate in witness and service, and to discuss the theological issues which still divide them. However, for others the meaning of the word "council" is determined by the councils of the ancient, undivided church; a council, then, is a "representative gathering of the one church", come together to state its common mind on specific issues of faith and life.[20] Thus the term "conciliar" could refer either to a process by which the churches worked towards unity, or to an event which expressed a unity which has already been achieved. There was not time to clarify the term, with the result that some churches never accepted that the word "conciliar" could be used in the present ecumenical situation at all, while others never quite saw what all the fuss was about.

Finally, it is significant that the power of JPIC to focus and unify the ecumenical social agenda is still being tested. At the heart of Vancouver's call for a JPIC process, and still hoped for at Seoul, was a vision of JPIC as an "umbrella" unifying diverse ecumenical programmes in the social and ethical field.[21] But it has not yet succeeded in redrawing the borders on the ecumenical map. For example, in the new WCC structure JPIC is not the overarching and unifying centre for social and ethical concerns which many had hoped for. It is, instead, one among seven areas in a large unit encompassing many aspects of ecumenical social action and witness. Strikingly the other six programmes, all on the same "level" administratively, continue important previous work in the traditional areas of development, ecumenical opposition to racism, issues of women and of youth, and so on. This gives the impression that for ecumenical social action in its institutional form, the former divisions and power centres remain largely intact. The continuing question is whether JPIC will emerge as a focal centre for ecumenical social engagement, or become one more — valuable, to be sure — "programme" among others.

These negative points are not intended to deny the importance of JPIC as an inspiration for ecumenical social reflection and action, or its crucial role in bringing churches into contact with Christian action groups and movements. Rather they are meant to clarify the place of JPIC within the whole ecumenical movement, and to sharpen our understanding of its relation to other parts of that movement. This suggests a review of that other classic and central ecumenical agenda, the search for visible unity. We will ask, in particular, what resources the search for unity has to offer for the churches' commitment to JPIC. If we focus on the Faith and Order movement it is certainly not because that is the only expression of the churches' search for unity; but it is a central one and, being lodged within the WCC, is that part of the unity movement most directly related to the JPIC process.

The search for unity: a call to witness and service

To understand the search for unity it is necessary to give up the stereotype — last valid in, say, about 1950, yet still dear to so many — of those commited to unity as quite divorced from the real world, concerned only with obscure theological points and technical issues of church doctrine and structure. In fact the past forty years of Faith and Order have been marked by the determined struggle to bring the search for unity into dialogue with the challenges posed by the world for Christian faith and for the churches. Above all, it has struggled to take seriously the divisions (such as racism and sexism) within the human community, and to take into account their impact upon the life of the church and upon the churches' work towards visible unity.

Here a consideration of the third world conference on Faith and Order (Lund, 1952) is instructive. The discussion of the "function" of Faith and Order first focused on the "essential oneness of the church of Christ", on questions of doctrine and worship, on difficulties and possible steps towards union.[22] But to this agenda the Disciples of Christ theologian Dean S.J. England added a crucial element: "To study the social, cultural, political and other apparently non-theological factors which affect the actual relationship of the churches to one another... and to consider the theological implications of these factors for their bearing on the move- ment towards the unity of the church."[23] Today this element, in even stronger language, occupies a key place in Faith and Order's by-laws.[24]

In response to this imperative, a long series of studies from the late 1960s to the present have wrestled with the realities of human brokenness and division in relation to the search for unity: issues of racism (in collaboration with the WCC's Programme to Combat Racism), the inclusion of the differently-abled in the life of the church, (most prominently) the community of women and men (in collaboration with the Sub-unit on Women in Church and Society), the intrusion of caste divisions into the life of the local church, and many others.[25] As noted above, this concern culminated in the study "The Unity of the Church and the Renewal of Human Community" and its summary and focal text *Church and World*. This has been the central point at which Faith and Order has grappled with issues of human brokenness, and with the methodological challenge of integrating the so-called "contextual" and the so-called "classical" theological approaches. For some the attention paid to these issues has been controversial, a "diversion" from our traditional and proper agenda. But the Faith and Order movement as a whole has affirmed this broader approach to the search for unity, agreeing that:

> ...churches today are divided not only over the traditional theological issues of transubstantiation or the proper age and forms for baptism but also, and often with more tragic results, by the alienation between ethnic groups, social and economic classes, and the sexes: the divisions of the world are, insofar as the church is a human institution, church-divisive realities. This did not mean that Faith and Order was shifting its attention to "non-theological" factors, but a new awareness that sexism and racism raise precisely theological and ecclesiological issues, and that work towards greater visible unity of the churches must also take account of these realities.
>
> The point is that the search for Christian unity, and the struggle to overcome the brokenness of the human community (a brokenness which leads to divisions within the church as human institution), are part of one and the same response to the gospel of Jesus Christ. The two must not be left to different "wings" of the ecumenical movement, thus reinforcing the old, destructive, tragic and false division between "theologians" and "activists". Nor is this a new theme for Faith and Order, but the direct response to a challenge already sounded in its by-laws...[26]

This provided the basis for a powerful critique of the "cultural captivity" of the churches to forms of injustice and oppression which threaten to impose themselves upon the life of the church as human institution. The last Faith and Order world conference (Montreal, 1963), for example, addressed the issue of racism in its working section on "All in Each Place: The Process of Growing Together", and asked pointedly:

But does the life of the church in each place assert the dignity of the human person as God's gift?... We are shamefully divided by racial prejudice and discrimination... In Christ there is no defence or excuse for the wilful continuation of groups, church meetings or fellowships which are racially exclusive. We therefore call upon Christians in their local churches to show the marks of Christian discipleship whatever the cost. [27]

This has been the basis for a developing vision of the local congregation as the place where one's doctrine of the church is "incarnated" in tangible form:

For it is here [in the local congregation] that the love, justice, reconciliation and "new being" offered by the gospel should be available; it is here that ecclesiology ceases to be an abstract system, and takes on a "human face", that its theological categories and truths become embodied in Christian sisters and brothers who incarnate God's challenging, enabling love and redeeming grace. It is not too much to say that the "quality of Christian life" within a Christian community is the primary test of its faithfulness to the gospel, more important than tests of doctrinal "correctness" (cf. Matt. 25:31-46, 7:21-23, cf. Luke 6:46-49!). [28]

And in a nutshell: "If the church is to be faithful to its calling it will need, as a community of shared faith, to exhibit God's justice in its own corporate life." [29]

It is essential that these concerns for human renewal not be seen as a sidelight for the unity movement, but are brought also into the heart of its reflection and work. They must become *part of* the theological and ecclesiological discussions on church unity. And this has happened to a degree which must be astonishing to those still controlled by old stereotypes of the unity agenda. Thus referring to the technical considerations of models of unity (organic unity, reconciled diversity, communion of communions), *Church and World* insists that:

the criterion by which the vision of the unity which Christians seek will be judged is nothing less than the radical renewal and fulfilment of the human community. The connection between unity and justice makes it necessary to ask of every expression of visible unity: "*Does it promote justice* in the light of the gospel of Jesus Christ, both within the church and the world?" And secondly: "*Does it foster the engagement of the church* in God's work for justice?" [30]

Thus the promoting of justice has become one criterion by which the search for visible unity must be judged. A true unity must include right relations and justice within the life of the church: churches may have come close to each other in traditional matters of faith and order, but if they remain divided, "in their living out of the faith and their ordering of church life", by racism "or other forms of human brokenness", then "such 'unity' is not yet the visible unity to which Christians are called by their being one in Christ".[31]

The link between unity and justice is so central to the future of the ecumenical movement that it is worth examining one more affirmation of their relationship. This comes from the united churches who, having moved from denominational separation through sacrifice to a new identity, are perhaps uniquely qualified to testify to the cost of the search for unity. In their most recent, fifth world consultation (Potsdam, 1987), they addressed courageously the continuing doubts about the "relevance" of the search for unity today. Their affirmation is so sound and nuanced that it deserves to be quoted at length:

> Many Christians today, engaged in their mission and service with the major problems of human individuals and groups, are unable to perceive any urgency in the quest for visible unity. Prolonged reflection on the theology of church, ministry and sacraments, so prominent in union negotiations, seems to them a distraction from pressing Christian duties. Members of the consultation declared their conviction that the quest for visible unity is related, and must be seen to be related, to the overcoming of human divisions and the meeting of human needs. This does not mean that the unity of the church is only functional: it is also a direct reflection of God's own unity and unitive love. Relating unity to mission, service and sharing the sufferings of humankind is precisely an expression of the love of God which calls the church into being, as the sign, foretaste and instrument of a new humanity in the kingdom of God.[32]

It is striking that this vision of unity and wholeness has not been confined to the unity of the church but sought also to encompass the created order. Already 25 years ago the Bristol Faith and Order Commission meeting, developing its programme on "God in Nature and History", affirmed:

> Christians should support all those responsible for nature conservation in various countries in their long-standing struggle against the pollution of air and water, in their demand for an afforestation which counteracts the denudation and erosion of vast regions, and in their plea for a policy of habitation which takes into consideration the much endangered biological balance of many areas. What these groups claim for biological reasons, the church has to support for basic theological reasons.[33]

The vocabulary is different from today's, and the specific issues may differ from ours, but the intent is clear: to call the churches to an ecological responsibility, and to do so within the context of their continuing search for visible unity. This call has been continued, and placed firmly within the context of justice, in *Church and World*:

> This new life in Christ and his justice should also be manifested in a new life-style of Christians and their communities. Such a life-style will express today an awareness of the injustice done to creation by unlimited exploitation, and will seek to support all efforts towards a responsible stewardship of creation. Such a life-style will be a contribution to a more just sharing of the resources of this earth between rich and poor, within the framework of a new world economic order. Such a life-style will in itself become a credible witness to the readiness of the church to be used by God as an instrument for the renewal of the human community. [34]

Furthermore, this view has not been confined to the churches and to the conventional ecclesial landscape. Already at its Louvain plenary meeting (1971) the Commission suggested "that the World Council of Churches explore still further the ways in which it can provide fellowship, support and guidance for those individuals and groups which are seeking new forms of Christian obedience for which existing ecclesiastical structures provide no opportunity". [35] This basic openness to the witness of Christian movements and action groups, and for that matter to learning from persons of other faiths or no faith, continues right through to the *Church and World* text, where we are reminded that:

> As Christians in different situations confront their tasks they become aware that they are not alone in their struggle. They are part of human communities in which the search for justice is urgently pursued and where often Christians need to learn from others outside the church what are the issues to be addressed. Indeed, Christians should expect in this co-operation to have their own limited vision of God's justice judged and renewed, and their theological perspectives deepened and enriched. [36]

The search for unity may prove threatening to those who are comfortable with the present divided state of the churches. This means that a serious struggle towards unity must expect opposition. The Montreal world conference faced this reality squarely:

> Unity is the fruit of Christian discipleship, and the latter takes various forms. A common protest against unjust laws which create or enforce racial divisions will make clearer the oneness in Christ... co-operative activities in

ministry and fellowship, when done *even in advance of consensus within a denomination or of the strict interpretation of canon law*, can promote unity. [37]

In view of the present emphasis on a consensus methodology in work towards unity (in which overt conflict is minimized as far as possible) it is striking to see how far, in the stormy 1970s, some degree of conflict was understood to be natural, even inevitable in this field. Faith and Order learned to speak of the search for "unity in tension". It was recognized that Christians, even as they worked together towards unity, might disagree strongly on specific ethical and social issues, and that some might be called to forms of witness which others would find unacceptable. Such witness, the Accra Commission meeting said in 1974, must not be sacrificed to a false understanding of unity which was concerned, above all, to avoid conflict: "An ecclesiastical unity which would stand in the way of struggles for liberation would be a repressive unity, hindering the just interdependence which Christians are called to serve." [38]

This survey has shown how the unity movement has, from its beginnings, wrestled with issues of ecumenical social witness and action. It is worth ending with a culminating unity document from the recent period, the text "The Unity of the Church as Koinonia: Gift and Calling" which was drafted by Faith and Order and then edited and adopted formally by the Canberra assembly in 1991. [39] This is the latest in a series of assembly statements restating afresh, for each ecumenical generation, the imperative and vision for visible unity. [40] It is remarkable how thoroughly the Canberra text, a powerful call for Christians and the churches to unity work through the 1990s, has integrated the imperatives which have come to be identified with JPIC. Thus it identifies church unity as "... a koinonia given and expressed in the common confession of the apostolic faith; a common sacramental life... and a common mission witnessing to the gospel of God's grace to all people *and serving the whole of creation*. It calls on churches to "take specific steps together... as they learn from one another, *work together for justice and peace, and care together for God's creation*". [41]

Of the classic assembly unity statements, Canberra's is by far the most concrete and specific in its challenges to the churches. Claiming the ecumenical movement "as a reconciling and renewing movement towards full visible unity", it calls them to a number of practical steps towards unity. Several deal with the interior life of the churches, calling for mutual recognition of baptism and the apostolic faith, and urging progress on recognition of ministries and appropriate exploration of eucharistic hospitality; but these are then related to an urgent call for the churches

> to recommit themselves to work for justice, peace and the integrity of creation, linking more closely the search for sacramental communion of the church with the struggles for justice and peace.[42]

Towards Santiago: an ongoing dialogue

The search for visible unity is receiving special attention as the churches look towards the fifth world conference on Faith and Order. Its theme — "Towards Koinonia in Faith, Life and Witness" — draws attention to the imperative for greater visible unity. Its key term "koinonia", variously (and always partially) translated as "communion", "community", "fellowship", has been used over the years to suggest a "dimension of depth" in the relationship among the members of Christ's body, pointing beyond the churches' outward structure to the church's source and sustaining power. As the New Delhi WCC assembly noted:

> The word "fellowship" (koinonia) has been chosen because it describes what the church truly is. "Fellowship" clearly implies that the church is not merely an institution or organization. It is a fellowship of those who are called together by the Holy Spirit and in baptism confess Christ as Lord and Saviour.[43]

The three sub-themes faith, life and witness invite a "harvesting" of the results of major Faith and Order programmes (baptism, eucharist and ministry; apostolic faith; and unity and renewal respectively) in recent years. But more importantly, they invite us to link ecumenical reflection (and also decision and action) on church unity with a wide range of crucial issues, not least those of justice, peace and the integrity of creation. In looking to the ongoing discussion up to Santiago and beyond, we want to mention three areas in which dialogue between the unity movement and JPIC might be especially fruitful.

Covenanting and conciliarity

The first area is the "unfinished theological business" identified from the JPIC process, namely the themes of "covenant" and "conciliarity" discussed above. Surely the nature of these themes is such that, for further progress to be made, *both need to be tackled within the context of the unity discussion*.

With regard to covenanting, the fundamental issue is ecumenical accountability.[44] Since the third world conference on Faith and Order

(1952) the "Lund principle" has reminded the churches that it is their *common action* which is to be seen as the norm, and their continuing divisions and separate programmes as the "problem", the distortion in our life together within the one body of Christ. As Lund put it:

> A faith in the one church of Christ which is not implemented by *acts* of obedience is dead. There are truths about the nature of God and his church which will remain for ever closed to us unless we *act* together in obedience to the unity which is already ours. Should not our churches ask themselves whether... they should not *act together in all matters except* those in which deep differences of conviction compel them to act separately?[45]

Today the ecumenical landscape is littered with agreements made by representatives of the churches, but not yet realized within the lives of the churches. Many have identified this backlog of unfulfilled ecumenical promises and opportunities as a major factor contributing to today's ecumenical malaise. As the working document developed in preparation for the Santiago world conference puts it: "In certain situations we observe a decrease of ecumenical enthusiasm and commitment to the goal of visible unity... in many places there still seems to be a reluctance to do together what is ecumenically possible."[46]

Is it time to say: for a while now, let the churches make no new agreements? Let them have time to put those which they have already made more fully into practice? At any rate, for the sake of ecumenical credibility a word as powerful and biblically-resonant as "covenant" should not be used without serious regard for its consequences in drawing the churches together. And that means asking about each "covenant" that is made for common action in the social and ethical field: what are its implications for the unity of the churches? We have seen above that the work on "models of unity" now recognizes that it has to take the churches' commitment to justice into account. Now those who work for justice must return the compliment, and consider the practical co-operation they undertake in light of the imperative for visible unity.

As for the question of conciliarity, this belongs even more clearly to the unity agenda. We noted above that the term can mean either a process of sharing through which the divided churches move towards unity or a representative gathering which expresses (and helps further define in specific areas) a unity already achieved. But in both cases *conciliarity is about unity*, and JPIC cannot claim conciliarity as its working method — much less a concept fundamental to its self-understanding — without exposing itself to the risk and challenge of the unity discussion.

The nature of unity

That discussion requires us to take a second step, and to ask about the nature and source of the unity which we are seeking. Since Nairobi it has been customary to think in terms of a "conciliar" unity. The renewed emphasis on conciliarity arose at the WCC's Uppsala assembly (1968) in response to developments towards unity within the human community. As, through communications and travel, "one world" seemed to become more and more a surprising reality, the church was challenged to reflect on its own distinctive understanding and experience of unity:

> In a time when human interdependence is so evident, it is the more imperative to make visible the bonds which unite Christians in universal fellowship... The ecumenical movement helps to enlarge this experience of universality, and its regional councils and its world council may be regarded as a transitional opportunity for eventually actualizing a truly universal, ecumenical, conciliar form of common life and witness. [47]

Uppsala's view of "the world" seems today to have been remarkably positive, with its reference to "secular catholicity" and "instruments of conciliation and unification" produced by secular society. [48] But since Uppsala the notion of unity, in both the secular and Christian arenas, has become more and more problematic. One reason for this is that, as the world indeed becomes one, the "oneness" we are being offered looks increasingly questionable, and the methods proposed to attain it increasingly dubious. Already at the first Faith and Order Commission meeting after Uppsala, at Louvain in 1971, a critical note was sounded about the "unity" being developed within the human community:

> ...modern technology has forced all mankind into a tight interdependence which constantly threatens freedom and individuality. The church's unity must be of such a kind that there is ample space for diversity and for the open mutual confrontation of differing interests and convictions. [49]

Today we would want to add a long list of unitive impulses (political, economic, social, ideological, valuational) which "the world" is only too ready to provide and which are urgently in need of critique from the perspective of the gospel.

A second, growing problem with the concept of unity is that many persons no longer find it a positive basis for their life and personal development, but rather a threat to their identity and individuality. Individuals and whole peoples increasingly demand that their unique, distinctive voice be heard, and while there is much good in these developments they yet pose enormous political, social and cultural problems. The working document for Santiago refers acutely to this "emergence of centrifugal, divisive tendencies among peoples and within nations... where unity and diversity are no longer seen as compatible".[50] It addresses realistically the impact of a divisive particularism upon the ecumenical movement:

> For a number of years there has been a growing preponderance of narrowly particularistic concerns (of churches or regions) over common ecumenical visions and tasks. This becomes even more serious where it is linked to a resurgence of nationalistic or ethnocentric tendencies as it indeed seems to be so in many parts of the world.[51]

The impulse to understand unity as uniformity, and to fear uniformity as the loss of identity, is making the churches' search for unity increasingly difficult. It has already seriously distorted the perception of the classic model of "organic unity", reading into it a rigid, monolithic quality which was never intended.[52] Clearly the recovery of a viable and attractive understanding of unity is essential today. The work on catholicity (diversity within the wholeness of the people of God) begun at the Uppsala 1968 assembly will be crucial in this respect.[53] (Here it is significant that Faith and Order's reflection on conciliarity developed in close connection with its study on "The Unity of the Church and the Unity of [Hu]mankind",[54] a predecessor of the "Unity and Renewal" study of the 1980s.) The experience of JPIC in shaping partnerships for reflection and action needs to be joined with that of the unity movement. And it may be that the wholeness and integrity of creation, seen in relation to all nature's luxuriant diversity, will give clues for our search.

The nature of Nature

This brings us to a third area for fruitful dialogue between the unity movement and JPIC, namely the question of how we understand and live in relation to the creation. JPIC has encouraged a strongly positive approach to the creation, and emphasized how "its mysterious ways, its life, its dynamism — all reflect the glory of its Creator".[55] Rejecting "the abuse of some biblical statements... to justify destructive actions towards the created order",[56] and an instrumental view of nature which has encouraged its exploitation by the human species at the expense of the rest of the created order, JPIC stands courageously for creation's inherent goodness. This is linked with other important JPIC commitments, for example to indigenous peoples who live integrally with nature.[57]

One pressing question is how ecumenical reflection can take into account other, much more problematic aspects of nature. We have quoted above the strong 1967 Bristol affirmation of Christian responsibility to care for and preserve the creation. Significantly, however, Bristol mentioned also the "ambiguity" of nature for human life: for nature produces not only the beautiful sunset but "the hurricanes, the floods, the droughts, the earthquakes..."[58] This points to the profound and difficult issues of divine power and goodness in a world which oft goes awry: if God is both good and the creator of all that is, why is there so much destructiveness in the created order? Why so much suffering and pain for God's creatures? While we may understand some suffering of human beings as the necessary consequence of their having free will, what about the suffering caused by an apparently indifferent, or hostile, natural order? And what about the suffering of animals, who live so largely within their programmed patterns of ancestral instinct? Or are these very questions inappropriate, a reflection of our chauvinistic focus upon the importance of the "human species"?

This issue will be on the agenda in Santiago. The working document, while affirming strongly the goodness of creation, emphasizes a Christocentric perspective as the key to grappling with the "ambiguity" of nature:

> Jesus Christ is not the Saviour only of the private and individual parts of human destiny; he is also the Lord of its cosmic vocation... The goodness and wholeness of creation is constantly threatened by death and decay, natural catastrophes and much suffering of created beings. The history of creation is marked by ambiguity. Nevertheless, because of the redemptive work of Christ, Christians expect the final healing, liberating and restoration of the whole of creation from the destructive powers of darkness and evil and look forward to the day when Christ is to recapitulate and consummate the whole creation in the eternal kingdom of God.[59]

This eschatological perspective enables us to celebrate the goodness of creation, and to face squarely its terrible aspects, by holding both realities within the framework of God the Creator's redemptive plan for the whole cosmos. *And it relates that plan to the unity of the church*, showing how our continuing divisions are judged also from the perspective of the integrity of creation:

> The division of Christians weakens their effectiveness in caring for creation; it subverts the sign of the unity of creation, and humanity remains without a challenge to its own striving... The churches by their divisions obscure the lordship of the Lord of creation. The problem is thus not only one of a divided witness before the world: it is also the problem of being faithful

before God to our calling to live as a koinonia of healing and caring in relation to creation.[60]

In search of a common Christological vision

In the end our best ecumenical future, I believe, lies in finding a strong and clear Christological vision to link the search for visible unity with the imperative of witness and service. Such a vision might well be rooted in the biblical picture of the cosmic Christ (John, Colossians, Ephesians), whose death and resurrection is at the heart of the divine plan of redemption for the whole created order and who lives today in the hearts of his followers. Some such Christocentric perspective was at the heart of the original, coherent ecumenical vision. This is shown by an analysis not of Faith and Order work, but from the Life and Work conference held at Oxford in 1937. It declared that:

> The first duty of the church, and its greatest service to the world, is that it be in very deed the church — confessing true faith, committed to the fulfilment of the will of Christ, its only Lord, and united in him in a fellowship of love and service.[61]

This text is not meant to claim centrality for the church, but to point the churches "to an intensely self-critical procedure" through which they are "summoned, in obedience to their one and only Lord, to become a fellowship of love and service. This fellowship, however, is nothing less than *the practical and ethical reflection of the unity of the church*."[62] This points us to the vision we need today, a vision by which we search fervently for visible unity, to the glory of God and for the sake of the world which God has made; and by which together we give ourselves in witness and service to others, and to the whole of creation, as a sign and foretaste of our final oneness in Christ, who is all in all.

This essay began with a story; it may well end with a prayer. The "Liturgy for a Service of Covenanting" observed at the Seoul JPIC convocation included a prayer for justice, peace and the integrity of creation, the fourth part of which calls us to community (koinonia). It begins by grounding that community in God's gift of salvation through Jesus Christ:

O God, who created *community* among us
through your Son, Jesus Christ,
his blood has made us one body
dependent on one another
so that we may help one another.
We thank you
that you love us as your people.

It continues with confession for our divisions and the destruction which they create, and then moves to a plea for unity:

> Through our selfishness we have divided the world.
> Our churches are separated from one another.
> We cannot take your supper together.
> Forgive us our sins.
> Make us instruments of your covenant, we pray,
> your covenant which is community
> and which demands solidarity.
> Grant us signs of unity.

It concludes with a call for new relationships, and for the power to shape that world which God desires:

> Heal our broken relationships
> through justice in peace for the whole creation.
> Give us the strength
> to follow you and be witnesses to your fellowship
> when other powers and loyalties divide us.
> You alone are our God,
> our Creator, Redeemer and Sustainer.
> Teach us your purpose for us
> that we may believe and live in reconciliation
> till the coming of your kingdom which is community. [63]

To this all those who work for unity, together with those who were at Seoul and with all who work for justice, peace and the integrity of creation, may surely say: "Amen".

NOTES

[1] Faith and Order Paper no. 111, Geneva, WCC, 1982. The text, sent to WCC member churches for official response in 1982, has become the most widely-distributed ecumenical text. Some 185 churches have replied officially, and literally thousands of "unofficial" responses have been received. Bishop Annobil was a commissioner between the WCC Vancouver and Canberra assemblies (1983-91).

[2] T.S.A. Annobil, "An African Bishop's Story", featured in *Church and World: The Unity of the Church and the Renewal of Human Community*, Faith and Order Paper no. 151, Geneva, WCC, 1990, p.11.

[3] This point is made with special sharpness in the working document for the fifth world conference on Faith and Order. See "Towards Koinonia in Faith, Life and Witness", draft of a working document (April 1992), Geneva, WCC, Commission on Faith and Order, 1992, III.3, para. 68, p.27.

[4] David Gill ed., *Gathered for Life*, Geneva, WCC, 1983, p.44. It is this element of contradiction, the way in which our divisions belie the message of justice, reconciliation and wholeness which we proclaim, that justifies *Church and World*'s description of them as "demonic forces that diminish the church's effectiveness as sign and instrument". See *Church and World, op. cit.*, chapter VII, para. 1, p.75.

[5] *Ibid.*, chapter IV, para. 31, p.48.

[6] Thomas F. Best and National Correspondents, "Survey of Church Union Negotiations 1983-1985/86", Faith and Order Paper no. 133, Geneva, WCC, Faith and Order Commission, 1986, pp.1-2.

[7] See the final version of the text in "Reports of the World Conference on Faith and Order, Lausanne, Switzerland, August 3 to 21, 1927", published by the [Faith and Order] Secretariat, Boston, no. 55, January 1928, pp.17-24. See also the earlier versions of the report of section VII in H.N. Bate ed., *Faith and Order: Proceedings of the World Conference*, Lausanne, 1927, London, SCM, 1927, pp.396-403 and 434-439 (emphasis mine).

[8] *Church and World, op. cit.*, chapter I, para. 10, p.4.

[9] "Now Is the Time: The Final Document and Other Texts from the World Convocation on Justice, Peace and the Integrity of Creation", Seoul 1990, Geneva, WCC, 1990, p.3. Also reproduced in this volume.

[10] See the "Act of Covenanting" and the four specific "concretizations" of that act in *ibid.*, pp.22-33.

[11] "Message", Seoul JPIC meeting, in *ibid.*, para. 7.

[12] "Now Is the Time", *op. cit.*, p.5.

[13] "Message", *op. cit.*, para. 2.

[14] "Now Is the Time", *op. cit.*, p.4.

[15] *Ibid.*, p.3.

[16] *Ibid.*, p.4.

[17] See note 1, and the summary and review of the official church responses to date in *Baptism, Eucharist and Ministry 1982-1990: Report on the Process and Responses*, Faith and Order Paper no. 149, Geneva, WCC, 1990.

[18] Aram Keshishian, *Conciliar Fellowship: A Common Goal*, Geneva, WCC, 1992, pp.2-5, especially p.4.

[19] *New Directions in Faith and Order: Bristol 1967*, Faith and Order Paper no. 50, Geneva, WCC, 1968, p.57.

[20] On this see *Conciliar Fellowship, op. cit.*, p.4. English has only one term for the two meanings of "council"; French, for example, uses "conseil" for the former and "concile" for the latter.

[21] "JPIC was envisaged at Vancouver as a unifying theme which "should be a priority for World Council programmes". A vast range of programmes (most already existing) was suggested for inclusion in its purview, from political ethics to the church and the poor to faith, science and the future, the perspectives of children, young people and women, the Programme to Combat Racism, etc. See *Gathered for Life, op. cit.*, p.255.

[22] Oliver S. Tomkins ed., *The Third World Conference on Faith and Order*, London, SCM, 1953, p.226.

[23] *Ibid.*, p.232.

[24] Available in Thomas F. Best ed., *Faith and Order 1985-1989: The Commission Meeting at Budapest, 1989*, Faith and Order Paper no. 148, Geneva, WCC, 1990, appendix I, pp.301-307.

[25] For a survey and interpretation of these developments within the overall history of Faith and Order see Thomas F. Best, "Beyond Unity-in-Tension. Prague: The Issues and the Experience in Ecumenical Perspective", in Thomas F. Best ed., *Beyond Unity-in-Tension: Unity, Renewal and the Community of Women and Men*, Faith and Order Paper no. 138, Geneva, WCC, 1988, pp.1-33. Of special importance was the "intercontextual" method, through which Faith and Order sought to incorporate reflection on contemporary Christian experience into its work on the unity of the church. See John Deschner, "'The Unity of the Church and the Unity of Mankind': An Appraisal of the Study", in *Uniting in Hope: Commission on Faith and Order, Accra 1974*, Faith and Order Paper no. 72, Commission on Faith and Order, Geneva, WCC, 1975, pp.85-86; and Mary Tanner, "The Community Study and the Unity of the Church and Renewal of Human Community", in Michael Kinnamon ed., *Towards Visible Unity: Commission on Faith and Order, Lima 1982*, vol. 2, Faith and Order Paper no. 113, Geneva, WCC, 1982, p.154.

[26] "Beyond Unity-in-Tension," *op. cit.*, p.13.

[27] P.C. Rodger & L. Vischer eds, *The Fourth World Conference on Faith and Order: Montreal 1963*, Faith and Order Paper no. 42, London, SCM, 1964, pp.85-86.

[28] "Beyond Unity-in-Tension", *op. cit.*, pp.19-20.

[29] *Church and World, op. cit.*, chapter IV, para. 12, p.42.

[30] *Ibid.*, chapter IV, para. 32, p.49 (emphasis mine).

[31] *Ibid.*, chapter IV, para. 5, p.39.

[32] Thomas F. Best ed., *Living Today Towards Visible Unity: The Fifth International Consultation of United and Uniting Churches*, Faith and Order Paper no. 142, Geneva, WCC, 1988, report, para. 8, p.6.

[33] *New Directions in Faith and Order: Bristol 1967, op. cit.*, p.17.

[34] *Church and World, op. cit.*, chapter IV, para. 27, p.47. See also chapter II, para. 29-30, p.19, and chapter III, para. 22, p.27.

[35] *Louvain 1971*, p.229.

[36] *Church and World, op. cit.*, chapter IV, para. 21, pp.44-45.

[37] *The Fourth World Conference on Faith and Order, op. cit.*, p.87 (emphasis mine).

[38] "Towards Unity in Tension", statement of the conference, *Accra 1974: Uniting in Hope, op. cit.*, pp.90-94; the quotation is from para. 10, p.93. The eumenical movement, then, is finally "dependent on the Spirit for the strength to reconcile within the one body of the church all whom the forces of disunity would otherwise continue to drive apart"; see para. 12, p.94.

[39] "The Unity of the Church as Koinonia: Gift and Calling", available most conveniently in *One World*, March-April 1991 (emphasis mine).

[40] The central texts in ecumenical discussion have been those from New Delhi ("all in each place") and Nairobi ("conciliar fellowship"). See W. A. Visser 't Hooft ed., *The New Delhi Report: The Third Assembly of the World Council of Churches, 1961*, London, SCM, 1962, p.116; and David M. Paton ed., *Breaking Barriers: Nairobi 1975*, London and Grand Rapids, SPCK and Wm. B. Eerdmans, 1976, pp.59-61. Also important is the statement on catholicity from Uppsala; see Norman Goodall ed., *The Uppsala 1968 Report: Official Report of the Fourth Assembly of the WCC, Uppsala, 1968*, Geneva, WCC, 1968, p.13. The Vancouver assembly referred to a "eucharistic vision"; cf. *Gathered for Life, op. cit.*, p.44.

[41] "The Unity of the Church as Koinonia: Gift and Calling", *op. cit.* (emphasis mine).

[42] *Ibid.*

[43] *The New Delhi Report, op. cit.*, p.119.

[44] A most helpful and creative approach to this theme is the pamphlet "Ecumenical Accountability: What Are Our Responsibilities to and for Each Other?" prepared by the Ecumenical Accountability Working Group of the Massachusetts Council of Churches.

[45] *The Third World Conference on Faith and Order, op. cit.*, pp.15-16 (emphasis mine).

[46] "Towards Koinonia in Faith, Life and Witness", *op. cit.*, introduction, para. 7, pp.7-8.

[47] *The Uppsala 1968 Report, op. cit.*, p.17.

[48] *Ibid.*, p.17.

[49] *Louvain 1971, op. cit.*, pp.226-227.

[50] "Towards Koinonia in Faith, Life and Witness", *op. cit.*, introduction, para. 10, p.9.

[51] *Ibid.*, introduction, para. 9, p.8.

[52] See the statement on "corporate union" or "organic union" from the second world conference on Faith and Order at Edinburgh, 1937: "These terms are forbidding to many, as suggesting the ideal of a compact governmental union involving rigid uniformity. We do not so understand them, and none of us desires such uniformity. On the contrary, what we desire is the unity of a living organism, with the diversity characteristic of the members of a healthy body." (Leonard Hodgson ed., *The Second World Conference on Faith and Order*, London, Student Christian Movement Press, 1938, p.252.) It is striking that the term "organic" is used not to suggest uniformity, but exactly to preserve a flexible, dynamic diversity! Archbishop Aram Keshishian notes the effect of this misunderstanding: "The model of organic unity had started to lose ground... mainly because of the fear that organic unity could mean, for some churches at least, the development of structures that might hinder the diversity of Christian life. The model of conciliar fellowship affirms diversity." See *Conciliar Fellowship, op. cit.*, p.21. But in fact conciliar fellowship was proposed as an explication and development of the meaning of organic unity. As the Nairobi assembly noted: "It does not look towards a conception of unity different from that full organic unity sketched in the New Delhi statement, but is rather a further elaboration of it." *Breaking Barriers, op. cit.*, p.60.

[53] "Since Christ lived, died and rose again for all mankind, catholicity is the opposite of all kinds of egoism and particularism. It is the quality by which the church expresses the fullness, the integrity and the totality of life in Christ." *The Uppsala 1968 Report, op. cit.*, p.13.

[54] For a careful summary and evaluation of the unity of the church — unity of [hu]mankind studies through the 1970s see Geiko Müller-Fahrenholz ed., *Unity in Today's World: The Faith and Order Studies on: "Unity of the Church-Unity of Humankind"*, Faith and Order Paper no. 88, Geneva, WCC, 1978, chapters I (pp.11-13) and II (pp.14-27).

[55] "Now Is the Time", *op. cit.*, affirmation VII, p.18.

[56] *Ibid.*, affirmation VII, p.18.

[57] *Ibid.*, affirmation VIII, p.19.

[58] *New Directions for Faith and Order: Bristol 1967, op. cit.*, pp.17-18.

[59] "Towards Koinonia in Faith, Life and Witness", *op. cit.*, chapter IV.2, para. 81, p.30 and para. 83, pp.30-31.

[60] *Ibid.*, chapter IV.2, para. 84, p.31.

[61] *Unity in Today's World, op. cit.* The analysis and commentary at this point by Geiko Müller-Farenholz is acute and very helpful!

[62] *Ibid.*, pp.15-16 (emphasis mine).

[63] "Prayer for Justice, Peace and the Integrity of Creation" from the "Liturgy for a Service of Covenanting", at the Seoul convocation on "Justice, Peace and the Integrity of Creation". In "Now Is the Time", *op. cit.*, p.54.

Justice with Peace

From Whose Perspective?

Oh Jae Shik

My intention in this paper is to explain my understanding of justice with peace, using the ecumenical process of commitment to justice, peace and the integrity of creation as a frame of reference. This process was recommended as a programmatic priority by the WCC's sixth assembly in 1983; and eight years later, the WCC reaffirmed at its seventh assembly in February 1991 the importance of JPIC as a programmatic framework for the future work of the Council.

Many national and regional consultations have been held on JPIC. I will draw in particular on the European meeting in Basel (May 1989) and the world convocation on JPIC in Seoul (March 1990).

I shall approach the subject from a local rather than the global perspective. I do not mean "local" in a geographical sense. Rather, by local perspective I mean the perspective of those who are involved as actors in the socio-political process. In other words, my basic interest is in the historical process and those who are actors in it. I may raise more questions than I can provide answers for. Perhaps such an approach will help all of us to raise more pertinent questions from the perspective of those for whom justice, peace and ecology are everyday issues.

• This is the text of a speech given at a seminar of the Life and Peace Institute in Moscow in May 1991 on "Overcoming the Institution of War".

Justice, peace and the integrity of creation

Theologically speaking, justice and peace go hand in hand. Peace is the fulfilment of justice. But historically speaking, this has not been the case. In the name of peace the cry for justice is often suppressed. The need for immediate remedies has often favoured peace and given it priority over justice.

Justice and peace issues are closely related to the question of who wields power at a particular time. It is therefore important to discuss the subject in relation to power. The role that power plays in determining priorities is clear, for instance, when the immediate stopping of mass killing is taken as a peace issue while the prevention of death from starvation is considered to be a matter of justice. Such arbitrary differentiations between peace and justice have distorted our priorities and the perception of urgency. The destruction of lives, whether it takes place immediately or over an extended period of time, is sinful. By the same token, killing through military action is ethically no different from killing through unjust economic practices. The argument in favour of a just war is not very different from the justification of the acquisition of wealth without considering its effect on others.

The final document of the Basel assembly calls for a new international order with just economic relations, lasting peace and ecological balance. But it has little to say on how we are to build and nurture the political will necessary to initiate such a process internationally. Maybe the European churches were modest, and did not want to prescribe remedies for the rest of the world. While I respect that, I still have some difficulty with churches in Europe turning their back on the rest of the world and looking only into their own backyards. The document is heavily Europe-centred. This tendency was challenged by people from the South at the world convocation on JPIC. While churches in Europe were advocating the abolition of weapons of mass destruction, the churches from the South were demanding that the economic systems of mass destruction be dismantled. The difference was mainly one of priority: which is more urgent for whom?

The same is true of the difference between economic injustice and environmental degradation. It is generally felt that the issue of the destruction of life from environmental causes is less urgent than that of death from starvation. While for some environmental disasters that are foreseeable in the near future seem urgent, for others the prevention of death from starvation and lack of medicines appears even more urgent.

The fundamental issue here relates to a gap in credibility. People in the North and people in the South have different historical experiences. One's perspective is shaped by one's historical experience and cannot be imposed on others, nor can it be easily shared. Unfortunately, common affirmations and promises are not sufficient to help overcome the gap between each other's historical experiences. Nobody questions the fact that we have to live together. But very few have given time to think through how our affirmations may be realized and made credible in a historical process.

The notion of what constitutes mass destruction also differs from situation to situation. For some, weapons that are designed to destroy lives on a massive scale are sinful, and therefore should be banned. But for others, from another historical situation, the reality of life is different. In fact, more lives are destroyed every day by an unjust economic system than by arms. Sooner or later we will come to realize the fact that ecological disasters will claim even more lives than an unjust economic system. In other words, it is too simple to limit the understanding of the mass destruction of lives to what is caused by weapons of mass destruction.

The framework of JPIC poses a fundamental challenge to our search for justice with peace. Each of the three components, justice, peace and the environment, is crying out: "The wolf is coming." In reality, perhaps, the justice part is saying: "The wolf *is* already in my house." The peace part is saying: "The wolf will *soon* be here." The environment part is saying: "The wolf *will come*." When the three are put together and there is the call for common action, what is the optimal line to draw to meet different historical needs? The question is not one of the authenticity of each call but one of co-ordination and prioritization for action. Prioritizing, however, will be possible only when mutual trust and credibility are established among the different perceptions of the time of crisis.

I will come back to this point later on. For now, I want to look at something a little different. In the seventies, there was a group of people working on models for world order — people such as Falk, Sakamoto and Kothari. I want to reflect for a moment on the discussion of this group. The purpose of the study was to envision a model that could be put into effect in the next century. Sakamoto listed in one of his papers the following as the core values for the decades ahead: ecological balance; economic well-being; communication development; human development; and peaceful change. "Peace is non-violent change," he said. It is a process of "dissociation of parties in conflict" and at the same time one of "association for common goals".

The vision of JPIC as it was launched in 1983 did not go very far beyond what the "new model" group in the 1970s envisioned. What impressed me in Sakamoto's paper is that he perceives peace as a dynamic process of denouncing and announcing. It is an act of building common goals. In the same vein, Falk summarized his sense of time. He said the 1970s was a decade of consciousness-raising on the issues of global challenge, the 1980s would be a decade of mobilizing and the 1990s one of transforming.

I have no difficulty in following Falk's time-scale. But perhaps an additional comment could clarify the issue. Although international discussions on a new world order have come to the stage of urging some decisive actions for transformation, there are still certain realities that require consciousness-raising which, in Falk's scale, were designated for the 1970s. Of course, I do not think Falk intended to divide the process so clearly by time-lines. Nobody really believes that history moves according to a fixed time-scale. Nevertheless, our cognitive faculty functions more easily on a time-line than in terms of space. Also, our expectations and hopes are on a time-line, thus generating frustrations when there is a lag in fulfilment. Whereas people in the North, especially Western Europe, want to move towards transformation straight away, people in the South feel that they have to carry on with consciousness-raising, mobilizing and transformation — all at the same time. I am aware that such differentiation needs further qualification and clarification. A call for common action worldwide, like JPIC, is easy to announce but difficult to act upon. For instance, a call for peace by the churches in Europe may not be received in the South with the same enthusiasm as in Europe. This does not mean that people in the South are not interested in peace. But their experience of peace and transformation is quite different. Repeated frustrations have driven them to take their own historical process as more central for them.

What then is justice when its authenticity is judged locally? How can we build a base for common action on justice and peace when the perceptions of the actors on timing and priority are different? One way to respond to such a question may be to stipulate once again our understanding of the common goals of action. As Sakamoto so rightly said, peace is not something waiting for an infallible definition but a process of action to make conflicting parties dissociate and associate for common goals.

Earlier I compared different types of threats to life. To reiterate what I have said, the basic issue for me is the question of political will which can implement our findings. The notion of people needs to be taken as the central reality of history in our discussion. Many would feel that it is difficult to establish "people" as a historical subject. For a long time, we have dealt with history from the perspective of powers and power centres. In such an understanding of history, justice is only for those who have power. Without power no one would even dream of demanding justice. Justice has been a tool of the powerful to defend their possessions and privileges. We do not need to go to Christian understandings of justice to criticize such a method. History itself has made its judgment. Recent changes in Eastern Europe have exposed the ways in which justice has been manipulated in societies that have claimed to be built on justice. At the same time, people have dramatically demonstrated their subjecthood in history. M.M. Thomas made the following observation on this situation in a recent presentation in India:

> I refer to the loss of the spiritual dimension in the secular ideologies which have been shaping European history in the modern period, as a result of the total rejection of Europe's religious tradition by those ideologies. As a result, the pendulum is swinging between atomic individualism and mechanical collectivism in the interpretation of human society, both of which are unable to see a human being as called to responsible personhood in community.

Thomas puts people-community over against individualism-collectivism. The affirmation that people is the subject of history has played a significant role in the process of awakening, mobilizing and transforming in Asia, especially during the period after the second world war. That affirmation marked a radical departure from traditional understandings of authority. It initiated a process of questioning the legitimacy of the power centres of the time and their claims to express the national aspiration of the people. There has been, however, in Europe a certain degree of scepticism and suspicion as regards the notion of people. The understanding of people, as experienced in European history, has been that of populist agitations which ended in the realization of absolutized power. "People" has been looked upon as an irrational and unpredictable entity. Instead, Europe has opted for the individual and has given high value to the rational mastery of self, the capacity to produce the maximum, and the discipline to plan. Can such an understanding of the individual be reconciled with the concept of "people"? Is it possible to build trust between the two?

Today we witness the release of human energies in contemporary history. One of the significant events in the post-war period is the emergence of common people as a political reality. People are aware of their own rights, and are linked to neighbours through expanding communication and transportation networks. They are moving to realize their destiny. Many governments have fallen through their attempt to suppress and brand people as subversive. Others have grown strong through getting the support and harnessing the energies of the people. Such energies, expressing people's aspirations, have manifested themselves in actual historical processes on numerous occasions, demanding a more just order. But many a time such demands have been frustrated. Power centres have not been able to create political space to engage in dialogue with people's energies. Although latent most of the time, the energy refuses to be crushed or to be compromised. Energy liberates people but power tends to dominate them. Energy is the countervailing force against power.

However, no energy or revolutionary force is exempt from critical or rational assessment. When it is being mobilized, revolutionary energy can in no time become power and start to revolve around the logic of power. Insofar as it remains in a political process we should not glorify energy as such. Nor should we put energy over against power. Nevertheless, energy mobilized properly does play an important role in correcting the wrongs of power, and in some cases alerting power itself regarding its wrongs. Energy thus manifested will take a variety of forms, all of which are historically and culturally conditioned.

The real issue in a historical process is that of establishing a rational framework that is wide enough to accommodate the revolutionary energies that are erupting. The problem we face is that as yet we have no system for understanding and interpreting people's energy. Because of this, people's energy is usually perceived as intrinsically hostile, unpredictable and potentially dangerous. How can people's energy be judged as legitimate before it is manifested in the form of power? How can people's aspirations be recognized as legitimate in the international community and be granted a status in the process of negotiation?

Justice in the economic world has been heavily tied up with the question of the distribution of resources. For at least the last three decades, governments in both the North and the South, and almost all international organizations, have tried to tackle the problem through rational approaches. Some progress has been made in certain parts of the world. But in general, most of these endeavours have not succeeded in controlling the rise of poverty and the number of deaths caused by it. People in many parts of the world are frustrated; and some are even agitating for revolutionary action because they feel all rational approaches have failed.

For a long time, economics has been seen as exclusively the business of science and the laissez-faire market system. In claiming to be a science, economic activities have claimed immunity from ethical and moral considerations. Consequently, the exclusive control over resources and the domination of others in the name of economic action have been tolerated. The promotion of justice in economic life, especially in the fair distribution of resources, will depend on correcting such wrong assumptions in the world of economics. Alternative schemes for the service of the entire human community need to be worked out. Along with that, steps should be taken to see that such a rational process bears fruit, building the political will and power of the people. I still believe in the classical political dictum that the powerful will not listen unless they are made to listen. Power centres, especially those which are linked directly to the economic beneficiaries of the present system, will not yield their power unless pressure is brought upon them. This means that the correction of economic injustice will only come from political action. C.T. Kurien, the well-known Indian economist, argues along this line when he says that "politics, interpreted as the power of people as against the power that arises from the control over resources, must be in command".

This basic approach applies to environmental issues as well. There are already numerous instances where people's action at the local level has stopped the destruction of the environment by big corporations which work with the tacit blessing of governments. In recent years, there have indeed been strong calls for building awareness and taking action to stop environmental degradation, issued by many governments and international organizations. While welcoming these moves, I still cannot help feeling a little sceptical about them.

It is expected that an Earth Charter will be adopted at the United Nations Conference on Environment and Development in June 1992. But unless there is an alternative power to put into effect such a charter, over against the forces that have been exploiting the earth's resources, it is bound to fail, as did similar attempts in the sixties and the seventies in the area of development. Such a call for action is comparable to the UN's call for the development decade that started in early 1960 and was repeated ten years later. I still remember the euphoria generated by the call. It promised that poverty in the world would be eradicated in two decades! Three decades and more years have elapsed since the call, and world poverty has grown not only in absolute terms but also in terms of the ratio of products to population. The problem of poverty is now left to international financial mechanisms and the governments concerned. No state and no organization, including the UN, is willing to assume responsibility for the hungry of the world. The poor and the innocent who endorsed the development decade are now left out in the cold. They have to deal on their own with problems of starvation and disease.

The issue of the environment is not in fact a new issue. It may well be a new entry-point into an old issue. It is another manifestation of the human greed evident in economic activities that assumes that the private acquisition of wealth has no limit. The proposed Earth Charter may generate a new awareness of basic structural problems and may even make some progress somewhere — which may be talked about as a show case. But my fear is that, with the general endorsement of the world community, the major corporations of the world, with the tacit support of governments, will use the Earth Charter as a new opening for making profit. Industries on alternative energy forms, new chemicals and tools, all in the name of protecting nature, will be imposed on the poor countries.

Given the international power game, I do not see any way of preventing such negative consequences. The arrogance of the US is greater now than ever before. Whether the United Nations can be strengthened and begin to act in a way that will win the trust of ordinary people remains to be seen. What can the ecumenical call for JPIC do? Can this process generate enough moral force to mobilize "local" powers for transformation? Will this process be sufficiently alert and mature not to fall into the trap of blindly blessing a process, as happened during the development decades?

Of means and ends

Again, I am reminded of the classical debate on the subject. Many sets of ethical guidelines as well as codes of conduct will be produced. But the real question is, can these recommendations be really effective? For instance, we can recommend reconciliation as an initial stage for building peace. Although the goal may be acceptable, will the weaker partner be really reconciled to the more powerful one unless the latter proves to be trustworthy? In many cases, reconciliation has meant the weaker surrendering to the stronger for survival. Furthermore, can trust be built without correcting the wrongs committed in past relations? So the issue is whether there is a stronger power or moral authority over and above the conflicting parties to reconcile them in such a way that justice is realized.

The same applies to the violence-non-violence debate. The matter is more complicated than the way it is presented in academic discussions. Quite often people are drawn into violence. They do not subscribe to violence under normal circumstances. Also, in most cases, violence is a response to previous violence. It is provoked. There are also people who, on ideological grounds, opt for violent means in their efforts to transform society. Once the option for violence is taken, the mechanics and logic of violence take over. For this reason, many denounce violence or violent means altogether. Some take such a stand on religious grounds, as an absolute pacifist position. I am not prepared to take such a position. Rather, I would like to look at the issue in terms of strategy or tactics. In terms of strategy, violent action must lead to positive results. To resort to violence in sheer anger or in reaction to preceding violence cannot be justified in terms of strategy. The premature use of violence will provide a good excuse for the opponent to use even more violent means. Also, the use of violence tends to create a vicious cycle of violence. Then, as I said earlier, the logic of means dictates the process rather than reason that should control the means used. Theoretically, I can tolerate the use of violence *if* it can eliminate the source of violence. Of course, it is a big *If*. But, there are historical precedents, although rare, where violence has been effective and therefore justified. In summary, I am not prepared to denounce all use of violence on religious grounds. My reservations on the use of violence are based more on the grounds of tactics and strategy.

Our discussion naturally moves on to the choice of the approach for transformation. Is a rational approach more moral than a revolutionary one? This is a hypothetical question because one who is not part of a historical situation may have difficulty in proposing remedies for those who are in it. Besides, a rational approach cannot exist in a vacuum. In a political process, when people are being mobilized, the opponent has to be portrayed as totally wrong and the people who are agitating for change as totally right. But rationally speaking, how can any political process be totally wrong or totally just? Political action in the streets is different from politics in the discussion room. Historically, rationalism has often been used by the power centres to defend their interests and thus prevent radical change. There is yet another aspect that we should not underestimate in this discussion — the tyranny of modern scientific reason. Having better access to data, scientific reason plays a major role in all rational approaches. With its technological know-how, it can easily eliminate those who have less or no access to resources of information. It will be futile, therefore, to use ethical or moral criteria on the choice of approach. It is the wielder of power who will win in this process. The real purpose is to bring to judgment the wielder of power.

The issue of legitimacy is important in a discussion on justice. For in the final analysis, in an actual political process, it is the nation-state which claims to have the final say on the matter of justice. At the present time, national sovereignty claims priority over the national aspiration of the people as the basis of justice. By the same token, the judiciary has the authority to administer justice in a national context, frequently over against the popular demand for a just order. Conflict is bound to happen when popular energy starts to challenge the legitimacy of an established system including the state. In a country where the principle of democracy is neither honoured nor practised, it is difficult to resolve conflict of this sort rationally. That is to say, in order to attain justice through a rational approach, there has to be a political system that will honour the consensus of the people.

Is an institutional alternative the answer?

What can the JPIC process offer to our discussion? After the historical turn of events in Eastern Europe in 1989 the political language of the international community based on East-West tensions is fast losing its credibility. Personally, as a Korean, I welcome the end of the Cold-War climate and the political rhetoric that went with it. But the virtual elimination of Soviet presence in international power politics is a matter of serious concern. Some people are arguing already for a uni-polar system around US military forces. They argue that such a possibility was demonstrated in the Gulf war. While Bush's "messianic call" may seem like a revival of Wilsonian idealism, it does not offer any tangible basis for trust. If its past actions are anything to go by, the US has not committed itself to strengthening the hands of the UN to work towards a lasting peace. Nor is the US prepared to move to change international economic and financial systems to better the lot of the world's poor. I suspect the US will drift between multi-lateralism and uni-polarism, at least for the time being. Likewise, the US will drift between the notions of common interests and of common values. At best, it may advocate a process of change rather than a structural change.

The weakening of political language may mean the curtailing of political space for the participation of the people. This will diminish opportunities for moral discourses and ethical guidelines. Our search for peace will still be tied up with military strategies. Our cry for justice is still at the mercy of the ad hoc temperament of the powerful. We advocate new values, but each one is isolated from the others. And each value has its historical ties, cultural colours and national or ethnic authenticities. We are still left in a temporal process over which we seem to have less and less control. Is an institutional alternative a viable historical possibility in which justice and peace can embrace each other?

Final Document

Entering into Covenant Solidarity for Justice, Peace and the Integrity of Creation

1. PREAMBLE TO ACT OF COVENANTING

From 5 to 12 March 1990, representatives of many Christian churches, movements and Christian World Communions from Africa, Asia, Europe, Latin America, Middle East, North America, the Caribbean and the Pacific met in Seoul, Korea to consider together their common response to the threats of injustice, violence and the degradation of the human environment. They summarized their findings in the following report which is addressed to Christians and congregations, to churches and movements, in the hope that it will contribute to strengthening wide co-operation with all who share the same concerns and commitments.

1. God — Giver of life

We have come together in Seoul to consider our common response to the threats the present generation faces. We have come because we share the conviction that God, the Giver of life, will not abandon the creation. We have come in confidence and hope, and at the same time in deep anxiety about the present situation and the prospects for the future. Humanity seems to have entered a period of its history which is qualitatively new. It has acquired the capacity to destroy itself. The quality of life is being diminished; even life itself is in peril. We are confronted by new and complexly interwoven threats:

— from entrenched and deadly forms of injustice: while a few of the earth's citizens enjoy unprecedented affluence and power, millions languish in crushing poverty, hunger and oppression;
— from universal violence in open and hidden conflicts and increasing violations of fundamental human rights: torture, extrajudicial killings and genocide have become features of our time;
— from the rapid degradation of the environment: the processes upon which life itself depends are being systematically undermined; already many species of animals and plants are lost forever.

The real danger lies in the interaction of these threats. Together they represent a global crisis. Unless far-reaching changes are made *now* the crisis will intensify, and may turn into a real catastrophe for our children and grandchildren.

2. God's covenant

As we face the uncertainties of the future, we remember God's covenant with humanity and, indeed, with the whole of creation.

• God, who is love, does not dwell in unreachable heights but is present in the creation as its sustaining power. God is alive in all that breathes and grows. Human beings, men and women alike, have been created as God's partners, called to witness to God's all-embracing love.

• Though time and again human beings refuse to accept — and even abuse — the status and role assigned to them, God does not abandon them to themselves. God stands ready to restore the broken communion. The sign of the rainbow reminds us of the promise: "Behold, I establish a covenant with you, your descendants and with all living creatures" (Gen. 9:9-10).

• Repeatedly people have been chosen to witness to God's saving purpose. Abraham received the promise to be a blessing to all nations (Gen. 12:3). God's covenant with Israel expected Israel to be a servant to the whole world (Isa. 42:1-7).

• God's covenants were fulfilled in Jesus Christ. The promise of a new covenant, to be written in the hearts of people, was realized in human history through Christ's incarnation and his death on the cross — the supreme expression of self-giving love. Through the resurrection of Christ, God's irrevocable yes to life has become manifest.

• By baptism we have been placed under Christ's covenant; and whenever we celebrate the eucharist we hear anew the words: "This cup is the new covenant in my blood" (1 Cor. 11). The sign of the eucharist anticipates here and now God's reign of justice and peace, the new heaven and the new earth which are to come; it is a meal we share with Christ who identifies with all who suffer injustice and violence.

• The covenant community is open to all. At Pentecost, walls were broken down. Through the Spirit a new community is being gathered out of the dispersion and division of nations, religions, classes, sexes, ages and races. Through the Spirit we all have access to God. The Spirit presses us to recognize and to rejoice in God's gifts in all people and in all places.

3. Discipleship in a period of survival

What does it mean for Christians to respond to God's covenant at this moment of history?

• Christ calls us to radical discipleship. The threats we are experiencing today are part of the price we have to pay for turning away from God's covenant. God's saving and healing love can only become manifest as we follow Christ without compromise.

• God's love seeks, in the first place, the weak, the poor and the oppressed. God never forgets the victims of human violence. We will experience God's presence and love as we identify with those who suffer and as we participate in their struggle against oppressive powers which dehumanize people and destroy the face of the earth. The anger and the rebellion of the oppressed are a sign of hope for a more human future.

• Given the complexity of modern society and the fragility of peace among nations, violent conflicts pose a greater danger today than ever before in history. War as an instrument for solving conflicts must be abolished. The church is called to be a force for justice, reconciliation and peace-making.

• God's covenant extends beyond the present inhabitants of the earth to future generations and to the whole of creation. If humanity is to survive, the rights of future generations and the intrinsic value of nature must be recognized.

• To give an adequate response to the global threats of today, the churches need to discover new ways of giving expression to their universal calling. They need to live and to act as one body, transcending the boundaries of nations and at the same time breaking down the barriers of injustice by which Christ's body is dismembered today.

4. Repentance and conversion

As we state these implications of God's covenant we realize how much we are betraying God's love by our witness and our life. The present impasse is of human making. If it is to be broken, a radical reorientation is required.

God confronts all of us with a call to repentance and conversion. Be reconciled with God, the source of life! But this call does not mean the same for all. Jesus' call to life took many forms — for the rich, it meant to get free from Mammon; for the sick it meant to believe in God's love and healing power; for the privileged, it meant to share wealth and power; for the downtrodden it meant to overcome despair; for the educated, it meant to renounce the pride of superiority; for the weak it meant to gain self-confidence.

Today, as well, Jesus' call takes different forms. We live in radically different conditions, and are still far from understanding the implications of these differences. But at the same time, Jesus' call is addressed to us through today's threats. Repentance and conversion have become essential for survival.

Who are we before God? We cannot find the answer by ourselves. We are accountable to one another and need one another to learn who we are before God. A global communion of mutual solidarity will grow only when we have learned to listen to one another, to see ourselves through the eyes of the other, to share our perplexities and to assess our failures together.

5. A community of hope and sharing

Conversion is the door to a new and firm hope — the conviction that the course of history can be changed. We are easily overcome by doubts: Has not power always had the last word? Are not victims inevitable? Are not war and hatred part of the human condition and therefore impossible to overcome? Is it not true that technological development has its own dynamics and therefore cannot be reversed and mastered?

Christian hope is a resistance movement against fatalism.

We want to share this hope with all people. We want to join with them in the same movement. We want to learn from their experience and from the hope by which they are sustained in their struggle.

6. Sing to the Lord a new song

This invitation means more than using a new tune. The Psalmist urges us to celebrate the new things God is doing in our midst. We are invited to be open to the future, and to interpret ever anew the signs of the times. As we reflected together at the convocation on what should be our response to God's covenant, we realized how quickly the world scene is changing and new challenges are emerging. There is therefore need to stay together in the process of mutual commitment to justice, peace and the integrity of creation, and to be prepared for a new vision, commitments and actions.

At the beginning of his ministry, in the synagogue of Nazareth, Jesus, quoting the prophet Isaiah, proclaimed the "acceptable year of the Lord" (Luke 4:19).

The expression refers to the Jubilee Year (Lev. 25) which was to be celebrated by Israel at intervals of fifty years in order to redress injustice and oppression and to recognize the limits placed on the human claim on God's creation. Jesus proclaims a permanent jubilee and thereby confronts the church with the constant task of witnessing to the demands of justice, reconciliation and the dignity and rights of nature.

The covenant community is a jubilee community in the service of all.

2. TEN AFFIRMATIONS ON JUSTICE, PEACE AND THE INTEGRITY OF CREATION

Introduction

In this world marked by injustice, violence and the degradation of the environment we want to reaffirm God's covenant which is open to all and holds the promise of life in wholeness and right relationships. Responding to God's covenant we profess our faith in the Triune God who is the very source of communion.

Our response to the covenant today leads us to make the following affirmations on urgent issues where justice, peace and the integrity of creation are at risk. They represent firm convictions that have grown out of years of ecumenical dialogue and struggle.

We make these affirmations as Christian people aware that many people of living faiths and ideologies share these concerns with us and are guided by their understanding of justice, peace and the integrity of creation. We therefore seek dialogue and co-operation with them, guided by a vision of the new future which is necessary for the survival for our planet.

We can make these affirmations only as we acknowledge our shortcomings and failures and commit ourselves anew to the reality of God's reign. This means to resist in thought, word and action the powers of separation and destruction and to live in active solidarity with the suffering people.

Affirmation I: We affirm that all exercise of power is accountable to God

The world belongs to God. Therefore, all forms of human power and exercise of authority should serve God's purposes in the world and are answerable to the people on whose behalf they are exercised. Those who wield power — economic, political, military, social, scientific, cultural, legal, religious — must be stewards of God's justice and peace. In Christ, God's power is demonstrated, in redemptive suffering, as compassionate love which identifies itself with broken and suffering humanity. This empowers people to proclaim the message of liberation, love and hope which offers new life, to resist injustice and to struggle against the powers of death.

> Therefore we *affirm* that all forms of human power and authority are subject to God and accountable to people. This means the right of people to full participation. In Christ, God decisively revealed the meaning of power as compassionate love that prevails over the forces of death.
>
> We *will resist* any exercise of power and authority which tries to monopolize power and so prohibits processes of transformation towards justice, peace and integrity of creation.
>
> We *commit* ourselves to support the constructive power of people's movements in their struggle for human dignity and liberation as well as in achieving just and participatory forms of government and economic structures.

Affirmation II: We affirm God's option for the poor

The poor are the exploited and the oppressed. Their poverty is not accidental. It is very often a result of deliberate policies which result in the constantly increasing accumulation of wealth and power in the hands of a few. The existence of poverty is a scandal and a crime. It is blasphemy to say that it is the will of God. Jesus came that we should have "life in all its fullness" (John 10:10). In his death and resurrection, Christ exposed and thereby conquered the powers that deny the poor their right to abundant life (Luke 4:16-21). God shows a preferential option for the poor. "The glory of God is reflected in the poor person fully alive" (Archbishop Romero). In the cries of the poor we hear the challenging voice of God.

Those whom society treats as "the least" are described by Jesus as his sisters and brothers (Matt. 25:31-46). While we support the need for diaconal services and urgent response to emergencies, we recognize in our time that the needs of "the least" can only be met by fundamentally transforming the world economy through structural change. Charity and aid projects alone cannot meet the needs and protect the dignity of the world's poorest billion people of whom women and children are the majority. The solution to the debt crisis can only be found through a just, equitable world economic order and not in palliative measures like the rescheduling of debts.

> We *affirm* God's preferential option for the poor and state that as Christians our duty is to embrace God's action in the struggles of the poor in the liberation of us all.

> We *will resist* all forces, policies and institutions which create and perpetuate poverty or accept it as inevitable and ineradicable.

> We *commit* ourselves to be allies of those organizations and efforts which are dedicated to achieving the eradication of exploitation and oppression.

Affirmation III: We affirm the equal value of all races and peoples

In Jesus Christ, all people of whatever race, caste or ethnic descent are reconciled to God and to each other. Racism as an ideology and discrimination as a practice are a betrayal of the rich diversity of God's design for the world and violate the dignity of human personality. All forms of racism — whether individual, collective or systemic — must be named sin and their theological justification heresy.

We reject the perversion of the language of human and peoples' rights to assert so-called "group rights", an assertion which is divisive and seeks not to liberate but to preserve economic exploitation and political privilege by powerful minorities.

Therefore, remembering the covenant of God who declares "All the families of the earth are mine":

> We *affirm* that people of every race, caste and ethnic group are of equal value. In the very diversity of their cultures and traditions, they reflect the rich plurality of God's creation.

> We *will resist* the denial of the rights of human beings who are members of exploited and oppressed racial, ethnic, caste or indigenous groups. We will resist attempts by dominant cultures and groups to deprive them of their cultural identity, full citizenship and equal access to economic, social, political and ecclesial power. We will resist the oppression and exploitation of women and children belonging to these oppressed groups. They are the ones who are the most painfully affected.

> We therefore *commit* ourselves to work against the forces of racism, ethnicism and casteism and to stand in solidarity with their victims and their struggles.

Affirmation IV: We affirm that male and female are created in the image of God

In God's image God created male and female (Gen. 1:27). This is the basis for a dynamic relationship between women and men for the transformation of society. Christ affirmed the personhood of women and empowered them to a life of dignity and fullness. Women with men, as "new creation in Christ" (2 Cor. 5:17), must work towards a world where all forms of discrimination are eliminated. Therefore, as we remember the covenant of God:

We *affirm* the creative power given to women to stand for life wherever there is death. In Jesus' community women find acceptance and dignity and with them he shared the imperative to carry the good news.

We *will resist* structures of patriarchy which perpetuate violence against women in their homes and in a society which has exploited their labour and sexuality. Within this we pay special attention to the most vulnerable women — those who are poor and/or black, Dalits, members of indigenous communities, refugees, migrant workers and other oppressed groups. We will resist all structures of dominance which exclude the theological and spiritual contributions of women and deny their participation in decision-making processes in church and society.

Therefore, encouraged by the persistence of women all over the world in their struggles for life, we *commit* ourselves to seek ways of realizing a new community of women and men.

Affirmation V: We affirm that truth is at the foundation of a community of free people

Jesus Christ lived a life of truthfulness. In living God's truth he came into conflict with the values and powers of his society. He communicated his message of truth to the people, teaching and preaching in simple language, and with images and examples.

People's abilities to communicate and learn are among the greatest gifts of God. They relate and bind individuals together into communities, and communities into the one human family. Communication and education in the service of justice, peace and the integrity of creation carry a tremendous responsibility for the future.

The prophet Zechariah says: "These are things you should do: Speak the truth to one another. In the courts give real justice — the kind that makes for peace" (Zech. 8:16).

Today, new technologies offer possibilities of wider communication and education for all. At the same time their misuse threatens the true purpose of communication and education. Ignorance, illiteracy, propaganda, misinformation and sheer falsehood face us everywhere; therefore, as we respond to the truth that makes us free (John 8:32):

> We *affirm* that access to truth and education, information and means of communication are basic human rights. All people have the right to be educated, to tell their own stories, to speak their own convictions and beliefs, to be heard by others and to have the power to distinguish truth from falsehood.

> We *will resist* policies that deny freedom of expression; that encourage the concentration of the communication media in the hands of the state or of economically powerful monopolies; that tolerate the spread of consumerism, racism, casteism, sexism, chauvinism in all its forms, religious intolerance, and a disposition to violence; and that acquiesce in increasing illiteracy and declining educational facilities in many countries. All this applies to every section of church and society.

> We *commit* ourselves to create means by which the neglected and vulnerable may learn and the silenced may make themselves heard. We will seek to ensure that the truth, including the word of God and accurate representation of other faiths, is communicated through modern media in imaginative, prophetic, liberating and respectful ways.

Affirmation VI: We affirm the peace of Jesus Christ

The only possible basis for lasting peace is justice (Isa. 32:17). The prophetic vision of peace with justice is this:

> They shall beat their swords into ploughshares,
> and their spears into pruning hooks;
> nation shall not lift up sword against nation,
> neither shall they learn war any more;
> but they shall sit every[one]
> under [their] vine and fig tree,
> and none shall make them afraid;
> for the mouth of the Lord of hosts has spoken (Micah 4:3-4).

Jesus said: "Blessed are the peace-makers" and "Love your enemies". The church as the community of the crucified and risen Christ is called to a reconciling role in the world. We have to discern what it entails to be makers of peace: the conscious acceptance of vulnerability.

In Jesus Christ, God has broken through the bonds of hostility between nations and peoples, and even now offers us the gift of peace with justice. No wound, hostility or sinfulness is beyond the reach of the peace that passes understanding. For biblical faith, true peace means every human being dwelling in secure relatedness to God, neighbour, nature and self.

God's justice is to protect "the least" (Matt. 25:31-46), those who are the most vulnerable (Deut. 24). God is the defender of the poor (Amos 5).

There can be no peace without justice. Such a peace cannot be obtained or guaranteed through narrowly conceived doctrines of national security, for peace is indivisible. True security must be based on justice for the people, especially for those most at risk, and on respect for the environment.

We *affirm* the full meaning of God's peace. We are called to seek every possible means of establishing justice, achieving peace and solving conflicts by active non-violence.

We *will resist* doctrines and systems of security based on the use of, and deterrence by, all weapons of mass destruction, and military invasions, interventions and occupations. We will resist doctrines of national security which are aimed at the control and suppression of the people in order to protect the privileges of the few.

We *commit* ourselves to practise non-violence in all our personal relationships, to work for the banning of war as a legally recognized means of resolving conflicts, and to press governments for the establishment of an international legal order of peace-making.

Affirmation VII: We affirm the creation as beloved of God

As Creator, God is the Source and Sustainer of the whole cosmos. God loves the creation. Its mysterious ways, its life, its dynamism — all reflect the glory of its Creator. God's work of redemption in Jesus Christ reconciles all things and calls us to the healing work of the Spirit in all creation.

Because creation is of God and the goodness of God permeates all creation, we hold all life as sacred. Today all life in the world, both of present and future generations, is endangered because humanity has failed to love the living earth; and the rich and powerful in particular have plundered it as if it were created for selfish purposes. The magnitude of the devastation may well be irreversible and forces us to urgent action.

Biblical statements, such as "to have dominion" and "subdue the earth", have been misused through the centuries to justify destructive actions towards the created order. As we repent of this violation, we accept the biblical teaching that people, created in the image of God, have a special responsibility as servants in reflecting God's creating and sustaining love, to care for creation and to live in harmony with it.

> We *affirm* that the world, as God's handiwork, has its own inherent integrity; that land, waters, air, forests, mountains and all creatures, including humanity, are "good" in God's sight. The integrity of creation has a social aspect which we recognize as peace with justice, and an ecological aspect which we recognize in the self-renewing, sustainable character of natural eco-systems.

> We *will resist* the claim that anything in creation is merely a resource for human exploitation. We will resist the extinction of species for human benefit; consumerism and harmful mass production; pollution of land, air and waters; all human activities which are now leading to probable rapid climate change; and policies and plans which contribute to the disintegration of creation.

> Therefore we *commit* ourselves to be members of both the living community of creation in which we are but one species, and members of the covenant community of Christ; to be full co-workers with God, with moral responsibility to respect the rights of future generations; and to conserve and work for the integrity of creation both because of its inherent value to God and in order that justice may be achieved and sustained.

Affirmation VIII: We affirm that the earth is the Lord's

The land and the waters provide life to people — indeed, to all that lives — now and for the future. But millions are deprived of land and suffer from the contamination of waters. Their cultures, their spirituality and their lives are destroyed. Peoples indigenous to the land and its historical caretakers have particularly suffered and still suffer oppressive separation from their land — by government policy and by violence, by theft and deceit, and by cultural and physical genocide. They await the fulfilment of the promise that the meek will inherit the earth. When there is justice in the land, the fields and forests and every living thing will dance and sing for joy (Ps. 96:11-12). Therefore:

> We *affirm* that the land belongs to God. Human use of land and waters should release the earth to regularly replenish its life-giving power, protecting its integrity and providing spaces for its creatures.

> We *will resist* any policy that treats land merely as a marketable commodity; that allows speculation at the expense of the poor; that dumps poisonous wastes into the land and the waters; that promotes the exploitation, unequal distribution or contamination of the land and its products; and that prevents those who live directly from the land from being its real trustees.

We *commit* ourselves to join in solidarity with indigenous communities struggling for their cultures, spirituality, and rights to land and sea; to be in solidarity with peasants, poor farmers and seasonal agricultural workers seeking land reform; and to have reverence for the ecological space of other living creatures.

Affirmation IX: We affirm the dignity and commitment of the younger generation

Jesus actively upheld the dignity of the younger generation. His saying that unless we become like little children we cannot enter into the kingdom of God (Luke 18:17) and Paul's call to Timothy not to allow anyone to despise him because of his youth (1 Tim. 4:12) imply a challenge to society to build human communities which, with wonder and curiosity, playfulness and vulnerability, with heart, soul and body, ensure the continuity of generations in the love of God. Poverty, injustice and the debt crisis, war and militarism, hit children hard through the dislocation of families, forcing them into work at an early age just to survive, inflicting malnutrition upon them and even threatening their survival. Millions of children, particularly girls, have no security in order to enjoy their childhood. The increase in unemployment, especially among young people, causes despair. Therefore:

We *affirm* the dignity of children which derives from their particular vulnerability and need for nurturing love.

We affirm the creative and sacrificial role that young people are playing in building a new society, recognizing their right to have a prophetic voice in the structures that affect their life and their community.

We affirm the rights and needs of the younger generation as basic for establishing educational and developmental priorities.

We *will resist* any policy or authority which violates the rights of the younger generation, and which abuses and exploits them. The human right of conscientious objection must be fully respected.

We *commit* ourselves to our responsibility to support young people in their struggle for self-actualization, participation, and a life of hope and faith; and to create conditions which enable all children to live in dignity, and where old and young share experiences and learn from each other.

Affirmation X: We affirm that human rights are given by God

There is an inseparable relationship between justice and human rights. Human rights have their source in God's justice which relates to an enslaved, marginalized, suffering people in concrete acts of deliverance from oppression (Ex. 3:7b). We recognize with contrition that we as churches have not been in the forefront of the defence of human rights, and many times have justified through our theology human rights violations.

The term "human rights" must be clearly understood to refer not only to individual rights but also to the collective social, economic and cultural rights of peoples (including those with disabilities) such as the right to land and its resources, to one's own ethnic and racial identity and to the exercise of religious and political freedom. The right to sovereignty and self-determination for peoples to work out their own models of development and to live free of fear and free of manipulation is a fundamental human right which should be respected, and so should be the rights of women and children to a life free of violence in home and society.

We *affirm* that human rights are God-given and that their promotion and protection are essential for freedom, justice and peace. To protect and defend human rights, an independent judicial system is necessary.

We *will resist* all structures and systems that violate human rights and deny the opportunity for the realization of the full potential of individuals and peoples. We will resist in particular torture, disappearances, and extra-judicial executions and the death penalty.

We *commit* ourselves to actions of solidarity with organizations and movements working for the promotion and protection of human rights; we will work for the acceptance and full implementation of human rights standards through effective instruments.

We further *commit* ourselves to work towards the full social integration of persons with disabilities into our communities through all possible means, including the removal of economic, religious, social and cultural barriers, (particularly ensuring access to buildings, documentation and information) which prevent them from fully participating in our communities.

3. AN ACT OF COVENANTING

3.1: Entering into covenant solidarity

Introduction

1. We have made the foregoing affirmations in responding anew to God's covenant. They represent the basic direction which the Christian

commitment to JPIC is to follow. Yet our response to God's covenant must go beyond the general renewal of commitment which is part of these affirmations. It must lead to concrete action out of renewed faithfulness to the covenant.

2. The following Act of Covenanting provides examples of such faithful action which is required today if the brokenness and violation of life and the division of our communities are to be healed. They translate the response to *God's covenant* into acts of *mutual commitment* within the covenant community. The building of links of solidarity around specific issues and concerns, of networks of communication and support, is the most urgent priority for action today. This underlines the fact that the human response to God's covenant is a corporate act.

3. The cause and consequences of injustice, violence and the destruction of the environment are intertwined. They affect people in an interconnected way. Therefore our form of action should also reflect this interconnection. This is one important aspect of the covenant solidarity into which we enter. The second aspect is this: our covenant solidarity is turned towards God in repentance and obedience and also turned towards suffering people and the suffering environment, so that it may be said that a real test of our covenant solidarity is the way in which we hold ourselves accountable to the poor and oppressed as well as to the whole of creation.

4. The three entry-points of justice, peace and the integrity of creation into the one struggle have to take into account the fact that poverty, lack of peace and the degradation of the environment are manifestations of the many dimensions of suffering which have at their root the over-arching structures of domination, i.e. racism, sexism, casteism and classism, which are evident in all situations of suffering in diverse and insidious forms. Therefore, as we project a common vision of hope as the basis for our actions in combating these issues, we should take seriously into account the perspectives of the racially oppressed and culturally dominated as well as other types of analysis, such as feminist perspectives on the causes and effects of poverty, violence and the misuse of creation.

5. Four areas have been selected for this specific Act of Covenanting as examples of the urgent corporate action that is required today. They express concrete commitments to work:
— for a just economic order and for liberation from the bondage of the foreign debt;
— for the true security of all nations and people;

— for building a culture that can live in harmony with creation's integrity;

— for the eradication of racism and discrimination on national and international levels for all people.

6. These four areas have been chosen because they are worldwide issues and are clearly interconnected both in their origins and in their manifestations. All four issues demand urgent action if the concerns of justice, peace and the integrity of creation are to be addressed in a concrete way at this time of crisis. They are, however, in no way exhaustive of our response to God's covenant or of our affirmation of our covenant solidarity. At the heart of our collective effort is the need to recognize the barriers and forms of oppression which divide us and to work for the complete eradication of racism and sexism in all our societies.

7. The fourfold act of covenanting represents a commitment which the delegates to the world convocation on JPIC have accepted in solidarity with one another. We have solemnly confirmed this commitment before God in the closing liturgical celebration of the convocation. We have thereby placed our act of covenanting in the framework of God's covenant. However, this covenanting action is not an end in itself. Rather, it is meant as the beginning of a process opening out beyond the participants in the convocation to the Christian churches, congregations and movements and even further to all people struggling for justice, peace and the integrity of creation, whatever their religious or ideological convictions. This act of covenanting therefore constitutes an open invitation to enter into this network of mutual commitments for action.

8. In this process of reception and confirmation, the directions for action have to be adapted to the given circumstances, which may lead to modifications. What is important is the interconnectedness and mutuality of the action, not the identity of the ways of acting. The act offered here is an example which provides a framework. Other covenants with a more specific scope have already taken shape at the convocation and have been witnessed in the closing celebration.

9. The emerging ecumenical network of solidarity links does need a certain support structure. This convocation looks to the WCC to provide the instrumentalities which are needed in order to maintain and extend this process. The WCC has grown out of an act of covenanting among the churches at the first assembly in 1948. It has described its calling as a "committed fellowship". These acts of covenanting therefore conclude

with an appeal to the WCC officially to make its own this ecumenical process of covenanting for JPIC, and at its forthcoming seventh assembly to assure its continuation.

One urgent request in this regard is the occasion of the five hundredth anniversary celebrations of the colonization of the Americas. The WCC should take up this complex issue and do substantial work on it so that an appropriate statement and a possible covenant may be prepared by the next session of the central committee of the WCC for the assembly of the WCC in Canberra 1991.

3.2: An act of covenanting and four concretizations

As participants in the world convocation on "Justice, Peace and the Integrity of Creation" meeting in Seoul, March 1990, we covenant together on the four areas that follow, and commit ourselves to raise them (and the practical issues of application which follow from them) within our churches, and to report on progress to the seventh assembly of the World Council of Churches in February 1991.

Remembering that God's covenant, which is justice and peace, embraces all of creation;

Professing our faith in God's promises for justice and peace on earth in its wholeness;

Repenting of our turning away from God's covenant for justice, peace and the integrity of creation;

Renouncing all idols of wealth, power, race and gender superiority and security which cause people to suffer and the earth to be dominated, plundered and destroyed;

Celebrating God's justice and peace and the mystery of God's creation; and

Opening our lives to respond in faithfulness to God's covenant with all living creatures, indeed, with the earth as a whole;

We make the following act of covenanting:

3.2.1: First concretization of the act of covenant

FOR A JUST ECONOMIC ORDER ON LOCAL, NATIONAL, REGIONAL AND INTERNATIONAL LEVELS FOR ALL PEOPLE;

FOR LIBERATION FROM THE FOREIGN DEBT BONDAGE THAT AFFECTS THE
LIVES OF HUNDREDS OF MILLIONS OF PEOPLE;

WE COMMIT OURSELVES TO WORK AND TO ENGAGE OUR CHURCHES TO
WORK:

*1. Towards economic systems and policies which reflect that people come
first*
This basic position implies that:
1.1   economic systems exist for humankind and not the other way
      around;
1.2   empowerment and participation of people and not accumulation of
      wealth/possessions are the basic organizing principles;
1.3   the idol of materialism should be replaced by respect for human
      beings, other living creatures and the environment;
1.4   the rich economies should accept a limit to growth so that resources
      can be made available for production aimed at fulfilling the basic
      needs of all;
1.5   no individual should increase his/her affluence at the expense of
      others;
1.6   economic and social policies are based on justice for all regardless
      of race, sex or caste instead of piece-meal, paternalistic program-
      mes of charity;
1.7   economic policies are based on people's participation and empow-
      erment at all levels instead of abusing people as consumers and
      factors of production;
1.8   economic policies reflect that justice for all people takes priority
      over financial gain;
1.9   equal access to education and meaningful employment for all with
      preferential opportunity for those discriminated against on grounds
      of race, caste and sex is seen as an indispensable foundation for a
      just economy;
1.10 the unjust economic system be abolished that forces women (and
      also sometimes children and men) into prostitution and other forms
      of sex industry in order to feed themselves and their families;
1.11 the basic needs of a society and its people determine economic
      and political policies — and not the economic values and
      interests of transnational corporations and international monetary
      agencies such as the International Monetary Fund and the World
      Bank;

1.12 we strive to establish accountability by governments, international organizations, transnational corporations, and other organizations like churches and church-related bodies, to all, especially those negatively affected by economic policies;
1.13 we identify and work to eliminate the structure of sexism that makes women and children the primary victims of poverty;
1.14 the economic worth of women's work be recognized and counted;
1.15 we actively search for a fundamentally new value system based on justice, peace and the integrity of creation that will guide political and economic policies.

2. Towards a church free of complicity with unjust economic structures and following ecumenical guidelines for the sharing of resources
This implies, among others, that:
2.1 churches reaffirm that economic activities, like every other dimension of human life, stand under the judgment of God;
2.2 churches recognize their need to be liberated from their complicity in unjust economic systems and recognize the principal role played by people's movements in the struggle for economic justice;
2.3 churches exercise stewardship over their income and possessions, e.g. lands, buildings and investments, and be guided in their policies by a preferential option for the poor;
2.4 churches adopt and apply the Guidelines for Ecumenical Sharing of Resources worked out in the world consultation on this subject in El Escorial, 1987;
2.5 churches support alternative production, trade, banking and credit systems which are based on justice, peace and the integrity of creation, and that they increase investments in the Ecumenical Development Cooperative Society (EDCS) by at least 50 percent over the next five years, thereby expressing the conviction that social return on investment takes priority over financial return;
2.6 churches and church-related organizations develop "economic literacy campaigns" to educate their members with regard to the way economic policies and systems work;
2.7 churches participate actively in campaigns to reduce the burden of commercial debt by at least 50 percent and total debt cancellation for governmental loans or other official debt;

2.8   churches actively support and participate in the WCC programme, Ecumenical Decade: Churches in Solidarity with Women (1988-98) and facilitate the networking of women.

3. Towards liberation from the foreign debt bondage, which affects the lives of hundreds of millions of people, and the establishment of a just structure of the international financial system
This implies, among others, that:

3.1   the international financial system be restructured according to the principles of universal accountability, equitable distribution and just reward for labour;

3.2   international trade policies be based on a just reward for labour and a just price for all commodities, and that the General Agreement on Tariffs and Trade (GATT) complies with these principles;

3.3   the rich share in the costs of adjustment policies that are necessary to eliminate the unbearable debt burdens of the poor;

3.4   viable and lasting solutions to the debt crisis are urgently sought, recognizing the fact that this crisis keeps whole economies in bondage, is an instrument for foreign domination, worsens the economic plight of women, children and other marginalized groups, ignores the fact that the wealth in the countries of the North has its origins largely in the exploitation of the countries of the South, prevents basic needs from being fulfilled, leads to environmental destruction, and is a threat to peace;

3.5   support is given to "the Year of Jubilee" initiatives taken by several churches and movements to work for the cancellation of the debt of poor countries;

3.6   we oppose all conditions on debt cancellation initiated by outsiders, no matter how well-meaning, and support only conditions demanded by people's organizations and ecumenical bodies of the specific debtor country;

3.7   support is given to the initiative to create an Ecumenical Fund to Combat the Debt Crisis into which those who earn interest could pay 10 percent of their interest earnings, and out of which activities will be supported which aim at exposing the causes and effects of the international debt crisis;

3.8   current structural adjustment policies which the IMF imposes on nations in debt be denounced as they result in the reduction of food available to the poor, thereby increasing under- and mal-nutrition, hunger-related diseases and infant mortality.

4. Towards the support of activities which aim at exposing the causes and effects of the international debt crisis and of those communities and organizations that try to create economic alternatives

3.2.2: Second concretization of the act of covenant

FOR THE TRUE SECURITY OF ALL NATIONS AND PEOPLES;

FOR THE DEMILITARIZATION OF INTERNATIONAL RELATIONS;

AGAINST MILITARISM AND NATIONAL SECURITY DOCTRINES AND SYSTEMS;

FOR A CULTURE OF NON-VIOLENCE AS A FORCE FOR CHANGE AND LIBERATION;

WE COMMIT OURSELVES TO WORK AND TO ENGAGE OUR CHURCHES TO WORK:

1. For a community of the churches which claim their identity as the body of Christ through providing witness to the liberating love of God

1.1   through practising our Lord's call to love the enemy;
1.2   through working for peace with justice for the whole creation, land, water, space and air, in which violence and structural violence are minimized;
1.3   through moving from the traditional doctrine in many churches of a just war to a doctrine of just peace;
1.4   through giving up any theological or other justification of the oppressive, threatening use of military power, be it in war or through other forms of oppressive security systems;
1.5   through actively promoting a culture of non-violence in which racism is overcome and the equal dignity of all races affirmed;
1.6   through the realization of a new community of women and men, overcoming structural violence and discrimination against women;
1.7   through witness to the peace of Jesus Christ by confessing that the loyalty to Christ is above the loyalty to the nation, and by declaring readiness to live without the protection of arms when the two loyalties come into conflict;
1.8   through developing and co-ordinating justice and peace ministries including a global non-violent service which can advance the struggle for human rights and liberation and serve in situations of conflict, crises and violence.

2. For a comprehensive notion of security that takes the legitimate interests of all nations and peoples into account; this common security has to grow from a realization of peace with justice and should include the defence of God's creation

2.1   through the creation of an international economic and social order that will enable all nations and people to live in dignity and without fear;

2.2   through the overcoming of the institution of war as a means to resolve conflicts;

2.3   through the rejection and overcoming of the spirit, logic and practice of deterrence with weapons of mass destruction whose use would infringe the principle of non-combatant immunity;

2.4   through the strengthening of the peace-making role of the United Nations and the recognition of the jurisdiction of the International Court of Justice.

3. For a halt to militarization, especially of the third-world countries

3.1   through the dismantling of military industrial complexes and through the stopping of the trade and transfer of arms;

3.2   through the withdrawal of military bases and troops from foreign countries;

3.3   through resisting national security doctrines, low-intensity conflict strategies and "total war" concepts and all other forms of destabilization;

3.4   through the building up and strengthening of democratic norms and institutions that will ensure justice and the rights of the people and enable participation of the people in decision-making processes.

4. For the demilitarization of international relations and the promotion of non-violent forms of defence

4.1   through a defensive, non-threatening and non-offensive posture of security measures and the development of civilian-based defence;

4.2   through radical reduction and eventual abolition of all nuclear weapons and, while nuclear weapons still exist, a progressive development of international control and thorough verification measures;

4.3   through reduction and limitation of conventional weapons and elimination of chemical and biological weapons;

4.4   through immediate cessation of all nuclear weapon testing and stopping the proliferation of nuclear weapons by strengthening the

Non-Proliferation Treaty (NPT) and ensuring that the nuclear
weapon states fulfil their obligation of disarmament under the NPT;
4.5 through unilateral steps of disarmament as well as bi- and multilateral steps and processes of disarmament;
4.6 through preventing an arms race in space through observance of the
Anti-Ballistic Missile Treaty;
4.7 through denuclearization of the navies of the world and encouraging
states not to allow to come into their harbours and waters ships
which cannot convincingly indicate that they have no nuclear
weapons on board.

*5. For a culture of active non-violence which is life-promoting and is not
a withdrawal from situations of violence and oppression but is a way to
work for justice and liberation*
5.1 through expressing and implementing the preferential option for a
peaceful resolution of conflicts;
5.2 through supporting the right to conscientious objection to military
service and tax for military purposes, and providing alternative
forms of service for peace efforts and taxation;
5.3 through overcoming violence in education, families, schools, at
work and in mass media, especially the pervasive violence against
women and children;
5.4 through resisting militarization as it specially affects women and
children depriving them of their human rights, dignity and health;
5.5 through recognizing and supporting women as builders of a culture
of non-violence and in their non-violent resistance to oppressive and
exploitative policies.

3.2.3: Third concretization of the act of covenant

FOR BUILDING A CULTURE THAT CAN LIVE IN HARMONY WITH CREATION'S
INTEGRITY;

FOR PRESERVING THE GIFT OF THE EARTH'S ATMOSPHERE TO NURTURE AND
SUSTAIN THE WORLD'S LIFE;

FOR COMBATING THE CAUSES OF DESTRUCTIVE CHANGES TO THE ATMOS-
PHERE WHICH THREATEN TO DISRUPT THE EARTH'S CLIMATE AND CREATE
WIDESPREAD SUFFERING;

WE COMMIT OURSELVES TO WORK AND TO ENGAGE OUR CHURCHES TO
WORK:

1. To join in the search for ways to live together in harmony with God's creation

Through activities such as these:

1.1   deepening our biblical understanding, rediscovering old traditions (e.g. the patristic teaching on creation) and developing new theological perspectives concerning creation and the place of humanity within it; through opening ourselves to learn from the insights of indigenous peoples and people of other faiths and ideologies, as well as from the traditional wisdom of women;

1.2   promoting a spirituality in our church communities which embraces the sacramental character of creation and challenges consumerist attitudes;

1.3   developing educational programmes which help people to uphold the integrity of creation and through adopting in our churches a community life-style and ways of using resources which express and reinforce a growing respect for God's creation;

1.4   acting together globally and locally with environmentalists, scientists, social activists, young people, political leaders, economists and others from different backgrounds and religions who are searching for just forms of society, which help maintain the ecological balance of creation. This co-operation could be enacted in many ways, one example being church participation in "World Environment Day";

1.5   protection and celebration of God's gift of creation by sharing the resources of the earth in ways that enhance the lives of all people. By rejecting over-consumption and promoting models which encourage recycling, provide adequate shelter and appropriate transportation, provide sustainable forms of agricultural and industrial production, and meet the basic needs of all people;

1.6   rejecting and fighting hierarchical thinking which puts one race above another, men above women, or people above the natural environment; and accepting the responsibility of constant self-examination needed for building a more harmonious world.

2. To join in global, local and personal efforts to safeguard the world's atmospheric integrity and quality

Including the following actions:

2.1   through keeping ourselves and our churches informed of the crisis at hand from damage to the chemical balance of the atmosphere and from changing climate patterns;

2.2   through responding to the warnings of the scientific community, the wisdom of tribal peoples and those most likely to be affected by the changing climate;

2.3   through creating, by way of ecumenical co-operation, specific policies and programmes that will mobilize Christians around the world in campaigns to save the stability of the atmosphere;

2.4   through participating in networks with other churches, environmental organizations, popular movements, scientific associations, and other groups committed to education and action to resist the causes of atmospheric destruction;

2.5   through supporting the efforts of international bodies such as the United Nations Environment Programme (UNEP) and the United Nations Educational, Scientific and Cultural Organization (UNESCO) to propose treaties for the nations of the world which will protect the atmosphere for future generations.

3. To resist globally the causes and to deal with the consequences of atmospheric destruction

Using measures such as these:

3.1   through reducing the emission of carbon dioxide by 2 percent per year globally as recommended by recent international scientific conferences. This would require the industrialized countries that create the highest emissions to reduce by 3 percent or more annually, recognizing the legitimate needs for sustainable energy expansion within the developing countries; in order to achieve this, a corresponding regular reduction in the use of fossil fuels is required;

3.2   through banning the use of chlorofluoro-carbons (CFCs) and supporting their replacement by alternative technologies and through international collaboration to make substitutes available within developing countries in an economically just way;

3.3   through combatting deforestation, preserving forest eco-systems and encouraging the reforestation and planting of appropriate varieties of trees as an act of contemporary discipleship and by addressing the injustices and attitudes which fuel the destruction of the world's forests;

3.4   through strengthening governmental measures to increase efficiency of both energy generation and use while encouraging transfer of environmentally relevant technologies from industrialized to developing countries so that the pressing need of developing coun-

tries for energy sufficiency may be met in a sustainable way. We
support a fossil fuel tax for this purpose, in particular in industrialized countries, as a necessary part of governmental measures;

3.5   through actively promoting strategies for renewable energy resources around the world as alternatives to increased coal, oil and gas
use in the future, and in strict opposition to the multiplication of
nuclear reactors, and to further disposal of nuclear wastes in the
lands and waters of the earth;

3.6   through proposing and supporting redesigned systems of transportation to dramatically curb atmospheric pollution and global warming
from this source and by committing ourselves to use public rather
than private transport and to restrict air travel whenever possible;

3.7   through the establishment of an international fund of atmosphere
solidarity supported by a tax on carbon dioxide emissions above the
world average, to be used for the transfer to developing countries of
technologies which are less harmful to the environment and to projects aimed at combatting deforestation and promoting reforestation;

3.8   through calling on corporations — public and private, national and
international — to implement responsible environmental practices.

*4. To call on our churches to lead in the indispensable reversal of the
thinking which supports unlimited energy consumption and economic
growth*

4.1   through strengthening public acceptance for necessary measures in
politics and economics to attain sustainable development;

4.2   through focusing on the ethical implications of setting long-term
goals which will include an equitable quota of fossil fuel energy
consumption for every world citizen;

4.3   through monitoring international negotiations regarding the
Montreal Protocol (1987), the Helsinki meeting (1989) and the
upcoming UN Conference on Environment and Development
(1992) — like the successful monitoring of the Helsinki Final Act
(1975) on human rights;

4.4   through encouraging bilateral and multilateral development projects
which include the full participation of those directly affected by the
decision;

4.5   through educating our parishes and congregations by special programmes and radically reforming the life of our church communities, through conducting an ecological audit for the critical
assessment of the design and use of church property, land and

resources with an understanding of shared community life and the integrity of God's creation.

5. To commit ourselves personally to promote and facilitate the achievement of these goals

5.1 through our witness and life-style: changing from private transport to public transport; reducing travel by air, wherever possible; adopting living habits to reduce energy consumption

5.2 through solidarity with those affected by climate change.

3.2.4: Fourth concretization of the act of covenant

FOR THE ERADICATION OF RACISM AND DISCRIMINATION ON NATIONAL AND INTERNATIONAL LEVELS FOR ALL PEOPLE;

FOR THE BREAKING DOWN OF WALLS WHICH DIVIDE PEOPLE BECAUSE OF THEIR ETHNIC ORIGIN;

FOR THE DISMANTLING OF THE ECONOMIC, POLITICAL AND SOCIAL PATTERNS OF BEHAVIOUR THAT PERPETUATE, AND ALLOW INDIVIDUALS TO CONSCIOUSLY AND UNCONSCIOUSLY PERPETUATE THE SIN OF RACISM;

WE COMMIT OURSELVES TO WORK, AND ENGAGE OUR CHURCHES TO WORK:

1. For just systems and policies which reflect that every human being is beloved of God irrespective of their race, caste or ethnic origin

2. Towards the implementation of the above-mentioned principles in the policies and practices of churches and church-related bodies

3. Therefore, in this convocation, in the presence of God

3.1 we covenant to confess and repent for our complicity either consciously or unconsciously in racism which permeates both church and society;

3.2 we covenant to fight against the violence of racism done to people in the first-world context;

3.3 we covenant to join actively in the land rights struggles of indigenous people as they struggle against racist institutions and policies which rape the land and resources;

3.4 we covenant to increase our efforts in the struggle against the apartheid system in South Africa which also undermines the integrity of the frontline states in Southern Africa;

3.5   we covenant together to use the occasion of the five hundredth anniversary of the invasion of the Americas, not for glorification but for confession, reparation and repentance for the brutal genocide and exploitation of indigenous peoples;

3.6   we covenant to support the continuation of a priority emphasis on the issue of racism, particularly the maintenance of the WCC Special Fund and the Programme to Combat Racism which provide concrete demonstration of solidarity by the churches with the racially oppressed;

3.7   we covenant to ensure that all racially oppressed groups, both in the North and in the South, are full partners in the ecumenical family in terms of participation and representation;

3.8   we covenant to convene a World Day of Prayer on Racism in which liturgical and background information on racism is provided to all member churches;

3.9   we covenant to develop faithfully in our situations the concrete linkages between racism, casteism, classism, ethnicism, sexism, militarism, poverty and the destruction of the environment.

Doxology
Having committed ourselves in covenant solidarity and
Mindful that we are stewards of creation
We join with all You made
To celebrate Your glory
And to sing Your praise.

Glory to God
Who in the beginning created all things
And saw that it was good.

Glory to Jesus
Firstborn of the new Creation
And Redeemer of all.

Glory to the Spirit
Who in the beginning hovered over the water
And who fills creation with Your love.

Contributors

Dr *D. Preman Niles*, formerly director of the WCC's "Justice, Peace and the Integrity of Creation" programme, is now general secretary of the Council for World Mission, London, England.

The Rev. Dr *Margot Kässmann*, a member of the WCC's executive committee, is working at the Evangelical Academy in Hofgeismar, Germany. She was a member of the JPIC preparatory group for the world convocation.

Dr *Marga Bührig*, a former president of the WCC, was director of the Boldern Academy in Zurich, Switzerland. She was moderator of the JPIC preparatory group for the world convocation.

The Rev. *Marc Reuver* is a Dutch theologian and historian.

Dr *Douglas J. Hall* is professor of Christian theology, Faculty of Religious Studies, McGill University, Montreal, Canada.

Ms *Brenda Consuelo Ruiz Perez* is a professor at the Baptist Theological Seminary in Managua, Nicaragua.

The Rev. *Rüdiger Noll* is consultant on JPIC with the Conference of European Churches, Geneva, Switzerland.

Ms *Priscilla Padolina*, formerly on the staff of the WCC's Sub-unit on Women, is involved in many church-related activities both in her home country of the Philippines, and in Asia.

The Rev. Dr *Kim Yong Bock* is president of Han Il Theological Seminary in Chunju, Korea. He was a member of the JPIC preparatory group for the world convocation.

Dr *Roger Williamson*, former director of the Life and Peace Institute in Uppsala, Sweden, is a free-lance peace researcher. He was a special adviser for JPIC matters at the WCC's Canberra assembly.

Prof. *René Coste* is professor in the faculty of theology at the Catholic Institute of Toulouse, and ecclesiastical general delegate of Pax Christi, France. He was a member of the JPIC preparatory group for the world convocation.

The Rev. Dr *Gennadios Limouris* is on the staff of the Faith and Order Commission of the WCC. His responsibilities include the study programme "Towards the Common Expression of the Apostolic Faith Today". He was a member of the JPIC preparatory group for the world convocation.

The Rev. Dr *Thomas F. Best* is on the staff of the Faith and Order Commission of the WCC. His responsibilities include the study programme "The Unity of the Church and the Renewal of Human Community", as well as work with the united and uniting churches.

Mr *Oh Jae Shik*, former director of the WCC's Commission on the Churches' Participation in Development, is interim convener of the WCC's Programme Unit III on Justice, Peace and Creation. He has extensive experience in organizing people's movements for justice and democracy in Asia.